complete

Reiki

complete

Reiki

The All-in-One Reiki Manual for Deep Healing and Spiritual Growth

Karen Frazier, PhD, RMT

ROCKRIDGE
PRESS

For general information on our other products and services or to obtain technical support, please contact our Customer Care Department within the United States at (866) 744-2665, or outside the United States at (510) 253-0500.

Rockridge Press publishes its books in a variety of electronic and print formats. Some content that appears in print may not be available in electronic books, and vice versa.

Interior and Cover Designer: Richard Tapp
Art Producer: Janice Ackerman
Editor: Andrea Leptinsky
Production Editor: Ruth Sakata Corley

Illustration: © 2020 Amanda León

Author Photo: © 2020 Tristan David Luciotti

ISBN: Print 978-1-64739-819-4
eBook 978-1-64739-494-3

R0

For all my Reiki students and healing partners.

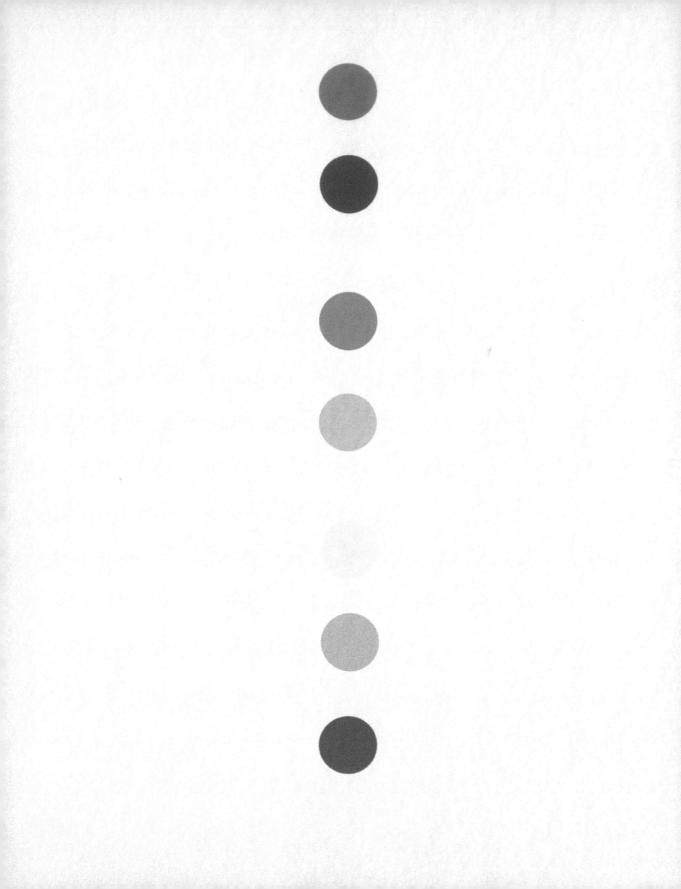

Contents

Introduction

Reiki exists in abundance all around us, and everyone and everything can benefit from its warm, unconditionally loving, generous energy. I've taught and attuned hundreds of Reiki practitioners and channeled Reiki both hands-on and at a distance to thousands. It is one of my greatest joys to watch another connect with the Reiki energy and realize what a powerful tool it is to create energetic resonance and bring balance to our lives.

I originally studied Usui Ryoho Reiki because I had been interested in studying Reiki for years, and it's what was available to me in my small Pacific Northwest town. I have studied many other forms of Reiki since my initiation into this healing art, but I always return to my roots of Usui Ryoho Reiki because of its simplicity, easy-to-follow system, and powerful love energy that it imparts to all who practice and receive it.

When my sensei, Howard, first taught me to channel Reiki energy many years ago, I had no idea what a major part of my life Reiki healing would become. I am now a Reiki Master-Teacher, and Reiki flows through me like blood flows through my veins. It is a practice I engage in daily, and virtually no aspect of my life remains untouched by Reiki energy.

When I travel, I send my dogs Reiki energy so they can feel its calming presence while I'm away. When friends and family experience any type of energetic disturbances of a physical, mental, emotional, spiritual, or situational nature, I ask if I can send them healing energy to support them in their life's journey. When difficult circumstances arise in the world, I send Reiki energy to the people involved, as well as to the planet, to provide energetic support.

In the morning when I wake, I reflect on the Reiki principles (page 25). When I meditate, I combine meditation with self-Reiki. I channel Reiki energy to my car every time I get into it to help it continue running well. I channel Reiki energy to my food, water, plants, pets, friends and family, home, and energy healing tools (such as crystals and singing bowls), as well as to the electronics I use and the world at large. Then, each night before I go to sleep, I reflect on the Reiki principles again. Finally, I fall asleep with my hands on my heart, channeling Reiki and love energy so they fill me as I sleep.

Although Reiki is ancient, universal energy that is accessible to everyone and everything, not everyone is aware it exists, nor do they avail themselves of its intelligent warmth. I believe the world needs Reiki and the loving, healing energy it provides now more than ever as we move into and through difficult times. Therefore, I've made it one of my missions in life to make Reiki accessible to those who want to learn to work with its energy.

This book, then, is part of that ongoing mission. It is intended to serve as a guide for people who wish to learn to channel Reiki themselves, whether for personal enrichment or to support the energetic harmony of all that inhabit this planet. This book can also serve as a resource for instructors who wish to teach Reiki, as well as for people who are curious about Reiki energy and simply wish to learn more. And, although working with Reiki energy requires an attunement from a Reiki Master-Teacher to channel it, this book will tell you everything you need to know so that when you are ready to be attuned to this beautiful and beneficial healing energy, you will receive your attunement with the knowledge of what Reiki is, how it works, and what you need to do to channel it to serve the greatest good of all involved.

PART ONE

First Degree Reiki

I practice and teach Usui Ryoho Reiki, the West's primary system of Reiki healing since the 1940s. In Usui Ryoho Reiki, practitioners typically start their journey through the three degrees of Reiki healing by learning and receiving attunement to First Degree Reiki, something I often refer to as hands-on or friends and family Reiki. It's a gentle, intelligent, loving form of healing touch that can benefit anyone who chooses to draw it into their bodies when a Reiki practitioner places their hands upon them to channel the energy.

In this section, we'll discuss everything you need to know to become a First Degree Reiki practitioner, including the history of Usui Ryoho Reiki, the hows and whys of Reiki energy, and the basics of channeling the energy through a series of hand positions. To channel all degrees of Reiki energy (First

Degree, Second Degree, and Reiki Master-Teacher), you must be attuned to that degree of energy by a Reiki Master. This section contains all the information you'll need to understand the nuances of First Degree Reiki. Once you've finished this section, you'll only need to find a Reiki Master-Teacher to provide the attunement (see the Resources section on page 212 to find a Reiki Master-Teacher), and you'll become part of a wide network of healers sharing Reiki with the world.

CHAPTER ONE

Reiki Energy

Once attuned to Reiki energy, anyone can channel it. However, it does help to have an understanding of what Reiki is and its benefits, how it works, and how it affects all types of energy. To that end, in this chapter I'll provide some background information that will be helpful for you on your Reiki journey. It's also essential information for those of you who wish to move further along in your Reiki journey to become Reiki Master-Teachers to teach and attune others to Reiki energy.

Universal Healing Energy

Reiki is the name given to a system for sharing universal healing energy (as well as to the healing energy itself) that flows through the practitioner and into the person receiving the energy. Channeled Reiki is a partnership between the person channeling the energy and the person receiving it. The person channeling the energy is called a *Reiki practitioner,* and I prefer to call the person receiving the Reiki energy a *healing partner* because the term conveys that in the healing process, the person receiving the Reiki is as active as, or more active than, the person channeling the Reiki.

Energy exists all around us. In fact, everything and everyone you can see or sense is made up of vibrating strands of energy held together by energy fields that we perceive as being solid objects. Although these "solid objects" appear to take different forms, at their very core they are all made up of the same energetic substance that underpins the entire universe.

Reiki is part of this universal energy, and when it is channeled through the practitioner and into the healing partner, it can support the energetic structures (chakras, auras, and meridians) that affect the health of the body, mind, and spirit of both the practitioner and the healing partner.

Because everyone and everything is made up of energy, it is essential that energetic flow remains in balance. Energetic flow can become overactive, underactive, or blocked for various reasons. And when energy does not flow optimally because there is either too much or too little, it can cause a lack of ease in the body, mind, and spirit. You'll often hear energy healers refer to this as dis-ease. Just as medical doctors attempt to work with disease in the body, Reiki practitioners and other energy healers work to balance dis-ease in the body, mind, and spirit to allow the optimum expression of physical, spiritual, mental, and emotional health.

When Reiki energy is channeled, it brings energetic balance to whomever or whatever is receiving the energy through a principle of physics called *entrainment*. When two objects vibrating at different frequencies are placed in proximity to one another, both begin to vibrate at the same frequency, locking into phase or *entraining*.

In the case of Reiki, the vibration of the Reiki energy flowing through the practitioner vibrates at a high frequency, and the healing partner's energy vibrates at a lower frequency. When Reiki flows to the healing partner, the two meet somewhere in the middle (entrain) to help balance the energy in both the person receiving and the person channeling the Reiki. This entrainment brings energetic balance and optimizes energy flow to allow the intelligence of the body, mind, and spirit to take over and create the conditions for optimal physical, mental, emotional, and spiritual health.

The Benefits of Reiki Healing

I like to describe the function of Reiki in a way that others can easily understand by drawing the analogy between the flow of energy in the body, mind, and spirit and the flow of electrical impulses through the nerves in the body.

Imagine that somewhere in your body, a bony structure is pinching off the flow of energy along one of your nerve pathways. For example, perhaps a misalignment in your neck bones is obstructing the electrical flow along the nerves that run to your heart. What would happen if, for days, weeks, months, or years, your heart didn't receive the proper flow of electrical energy from your nerves? Over time, your heart would weaken and begin to malfunction until it started to manifest symptoms, which are signals your body sends telling you something is wrong. By the time your body started sending these signals, it's likely your heart wouldn't be functioning as well as it did when it was receiving electrical impulses properly.

Therefore, the best way to treat the heart malfunction would be to remove the impingement on the nerve and restore proper flow of electrical impulses. Once nerve flow was properly restored, the intelligence of the body could take over and healing would begin.

Reiki is the energetic equivalent of this for your body, mind, and spirit and its main benefit is to restore the proper balanced energy flow to allow the intelligence of your body, mind, and spirit to create the conditions for healing. In short, Reiki balances your energetics so that the wisdom of body, mind, and spirit can restore well-being.

The Reiki Origin Story

First Degree Reiki practitioners learn of the origins of Reiki during their training. As Reiki practitioners, we feel deep respect for how Reiki came from Japan and into the West and for the people who brought us this gentle and intelligent system of healing.

Although Usui Ryoho Reiki is considered a reasonably modern healing practice, originating in Japan in the 1920s, the energy used in Reiki is as ancient as the universe itself. However, our story, which is the history of the Western practice of Reiki, begins in Japan in the 1920s with Dr. Mikao Usui, also known as Usui Sensei.

Japanese Practitioners Before Usui

We start our story with Usui Sensei because it is his system that was spread in the West, so a significant portion of Western Reiki practitioners can trace their lineage back to his teachings. However, even before Dr. Usui developed his system, there is evidence of at least four forms of energy healing called Reiki being practiced in Japan, and some evidence suggests Reiki has been practiced in some form or another for thousands of years. It is likely Dr. Usui built his system on the foundations of thousands of years of energy healing practices in Japan.

MIKAO USUI

Mikao Usui was a Buddhist monk from a wealthy family. He had a deep interest in medicine and in finding a form of energy healing that could bring balance of the body, mind, and spirit. While he was studying in the monastery, Usui Sensei ascended Mount Kurama, where he meditated, fasted, and prayed in a cave for 21 days. On the 21st day, he had a spiritual awakening. He saw Sanskrit symbols appear on the cave wall and was inspired to develop a system of energy healing that we know today as Usui Ryoho Reiki. In 1922, he founded a Reiki clinic and school in Tokyo. It was there that he trained a number of Japanese practitioners, including Dr. Chujiro Hayashi.

CHUJIRO HAYASHI

Chujiro Hayashi was a medical doctor and naval officer who learned Reiki at Dr. Usui's Tokyo clinic and school. After learning from Usui Sensei, Dr. Hayashi also developed a series of hand positions that enhanced the Reiki treatments, and he began teaching and practicing Reiki at a clinic in Tokyo. He trained several Japanese Reiki practitioners, as well as a Japanese American woman from Hawaii named Mrs. Hawayo Takata. After visiting Mrs. Takata in Hawaii in the 1940s, Dr. Hayashi returned to Japan. The government wanted him to share secrets from his experiences in America and what he had learned there. Dr. Hayashi chose *seppuku* (ritual suicide), which was considered an honorable death, rather than comply with what the government was asking.

HAWAYO TAKATA

Mrs. Takata is responsible for the spread of Reiki in the West. She further enhanced Dr. Usui's and Dr. Hayashi's treatments by adding a system of hand placements she called *Foundation Treatment* (the hand positions taught today). To honor the Reiki traditions and the work of Drs. Usui and Hayashi, Mrs. Takata was extremely careful about who she taught Reiki to and how she taught it. She insisted Reiki be taught as an oral tradition—humankind's first and most ubiquitous form of communication—and charged $10,000 to teach and attune Reiki practitioners to honor the traditions she learned. In her lifetime, Mrs. Takata trained and attuned 22 Reiki practitioners in the West, and all Usui Ryoho Reiki practitioners can trace their lineage back through Mrs. Takata to Drs. Hayashi and Usui.

Today, there are thousands of Reiki practitioners throughout the West, and Reiki continues to expand in amazing ways. In fact, it's gone mainstream. Many health care practitioners—such as massage therapists, nurses, and physical therapists—add Reiki to complement their healing arts. Reiki is also available in some hospitals, as well as in nursing homes and hospices.

Reiki Healing Traditions

Modern Reiki is a mix of Japanese, Western, and nontraditional forms of Reiki. Many Western Reiki practitioners follow the system originally taught by Mrs. Takata. Some follow her systems very strictly, whereas others branched off and made Reiki their own. For example, Reiki is no longer considered strictly an oral tradition. Both Dr. Hayashi and Dr. Usui provided written materials about Reiki to their students, and many Reiki Master-Teachers today (including me) feel it is beneficial to supplement oral and hands-on teachings with written materials. In this way, Reiki has become a blend of old and new healing traditions.

The Usui Ryoho Reiki Healing System

The Usui Ryoho Reiki healing system offers the following:

- 12 hand positions for healing others
- 13 hand positions for healing self
- Three degrees of Reiki (First Degree, or Shoden; Second Degree, or Okuden; and Master-Teacher Degree, or Shinpiden)
- Three traditional healing symbols in Second Degree Reiki for physical, emotional, spiritual, and distance healing
- One Master symbol for Master-Teacher Degree Reiki
- A Reiki lineage tracing back through Mrs. Takata, Dr. Hayashi, and Usui Sensei

Nontraditional Reiki

Other systems of Reiki have made it to the West as well. Although they use the same energy and have similar principles to Usui Ryoho Reiki, they may rely on different symbols and processes during Reiki treatments. Some less common forms of Reiki you might come across in the West include Usui Shiki Ryoho Reiki, Karuna Ki Reiki, Saku Reiki, Raku Reiki, and many others.

Though all traditions use the same energy, some are older systems that come directly from Japan, and others are Reiki systems that have been developed in the West relying on different practices, hand positions, intentions, and more. Some are even a hybrid of Reiki and other energy healing practices.

I urge you to find the system of Reiki that resonates most for you; none is inherently wrong or right, as Reiki is an intelligent energy that goes where it is needed and serves the greatest good regardless of the system of delivery. Therefore, as a Reiki practitioner, you are free to select the system of Reiki that makes the most sense to you.

Chakra Healing and Related Conditions

Although you don't need to know every aspect of energy anatomy (also called *subtle anatomy*) to practice Reiki, having a basic understanding of the chakra system can help you when you work with your own healing and with healing partners.

Human beings are a combination of body, mind, emotions, and spirit. When considering human health, it is impossible to separate one of these from the other three. All are interconnected and affect how health manifests in your body. Your body and mind are of the *physical body*. Your emotions and spirit are of the *etheric (spiritual) body*. Your energy anatomy—consisting of your *meridians, chakras,* and *aura*—is the point of energetic connection between your physical body and your etheric body. Energetic balance of your subtle anatomy is essential for health of the body, mind, emotions, and spirit.

Though each part of your subtle anatomy affects your overall health picture, chakras are the easiest to visualize and understand, which is why I tend to teach them as part of the Reiki curriculum. Your chakras are energetic centers that exist to connect your physical body to your spiritual body. They are visualized as spinning wheels of colored light that run roughly along your spinal column. Each chakra vibrates at the frequency of a different color, and each affects and is affected by various aspects of physical, mental, emotional, and spiritual health.

Root Chakra · Muladhara

LOCATION: Base of your spine/tailbone

COLOR: Red

Your root chakra—also known as the first chakra or by its Sanskrit name Muladhara—is located at the base of your spine near your tailbone. This is the energetic center of grounding, safety, and security. When this chakra is out of balance, you may feel insecure or unsafe. You may struggle with meeting your basic safety and security needs. Physically, imbalances may manifest in issues such as depression, autoimmune disease, and physical problems of the legs, knees, feet, and toes.

Tips for Keeping It Healthy

▶ Practice grounding. Visualize roots growing out of your feet into the Earth and spend time with your bare feet connected to the Earth.

▶ Channel Reiki or healing energy to your root chakra.

▶ Work with red or black crystals such as garnet and black tourmaline.

▶ Visualize a red wheel of light spinning in your root chakra, and imagine bright white light passing easily through the spinning chakra.

▶ Enjoy root vegetables such as potatoes, carrots, or turnips to support the energy of this chakra.

▶ Practice grounding movement, such as child's pose in yoga.

▶ Diffuse grounding essential oils, such as patchouli or cinnamon.

Sacral Chakra · Svadhishthana

LOCATION: About a handbreadth below your navel

COLOR: Orange

Your sacral chakra—also known as the second chakra or by its Sanskrit name Svadhishthana—is located in the center of your body about a handbreadth below your navel. This is the energetic center of confidence, motivation, prosperity, and sexuality. When this chakra is out of balance, you may experience issues such as low libido, financial problems, and blocked creativity. Physically, imbalances will often manifest in your intestinal and lower abdominal organs and sexual organs as well as your hips.

Tips for Keeping It Healthy

- Dance. Dancing of all types opens up sacral chakra energy, especially when it's unselfconscious dancing.
- Channel Reiki or healing energy to your sacral chakra.
- Work with orange or brown crystals such as carnelian and smoky quartz.
- Visualize an orange wheel of light spinning in your sacral chakra, and imagine bright white light passing easily through the spinning chakra.
- Orange natural foods such as carrots, orange peppers, and orange fruits are perfect for balancing this chakra.
- Yoga poses that open the hips, such as pigeon pose or seated forward bend, can help balance this chakra.
- Diffuse essential oils that support the sacral chakra, such as orange or grapefruit.

Solar Plexus Chakra · Manipura

LOCATION: Base of your sternum
COLOR: Yellow

Your solar plexus chakra—also known as the third chakra or by its Sanskrit name Manipura—is located at the base of your sternum near the xiphoid process. This is the energetic center of self, ego, willpower, and personal power. When this chakra is out of balance, you may have poor boundaries, have a poor sense of self, or be overly ego-invested. Physically, imbalances may affect your adrenal glands, kidneys, gall-bladder, liver, and other abdominal organs as well as your rib cage and middle back.

Tips for Keeping It Healthy

▶ Practice physical balance. Engaging in exercises of upright physical balance such as walking on a balance beam or Hula-Hooping can activate and engage this chakra to bring balance.

▶ Channel Reiki or healing energy to your solar plexus chakra.

▶ Work with yellow or gold gemstones such as yellow tigers eye, citrine, or pyrite.

▶ Visualize a yellow wheel of light spinning in your solar plexus chakra, and imagine bright white light passing easily through the spinning chakra.

▶ Consume yellow or golden foods and spices such as ginger, bananas, and turmeric to help bring balance to the solar plexus chakra.

▶ Yoga balancing movements, such as tree pose, boat pose, and warrior pose, are excellent for balancing solar plexus energy.

▶ Diffuse essential oils that support the solar plexus, such as lemon or ginger.

Heart Chakra · Anahata

LOCATION: Center of your chest

COLOR: Green

Your heart chakra—also known as the fourth chakra or by its Sanskrit name Anahata—is located in the center of your chest. This is the energetic center of love, and it serves to bridge the physical and the etheric. When this chakra is out of balance, you may experience anger, bitterness, or unwillingness to forgive. Physically, imbalances may manifest in the heart, lungs, circulatory system, and chest region.

Tips for Keeping It Healthy

▸ Repetitive aerobic activity, such as walking, running, and swimming, can help keep heart energy balanced.

▸ Channel Reiki or healing energy to your heart chakra.

▸ Work with pink or green gemstones such as emerald and rose quartz.

▸ Visualize a green wheel of light spinning in your heart chakra, and imagine bright white light passing easily through the spinning chakra.

▸ Enjoy green fruits and vegetables such as kale, spinach, or limes to support the energy of this chakra.

▸ Practice heart-opening yoga asanas, such as upward dog, cobra, and bow pose.

▸ Diffuse heart energy essential oils, such as rose and jasmine.

Throat Chakra · Vishuddha

LOCATION: Center of your throat

COLOR: Blue

Your throat chakra—also known as the fifth chakra or by its Sanskrit name Vishuddha—is located at the center of your throat over your thyroid. This is the energetic center of truth, integrity, and self-expression. When this chakra is out of balance, you may be highly critical or judgmental, or you may feel you are unable to express yourself. Physically, imbalances may manifest in issues of the throat, thyroid, jaw, mouth, shoulders, teeth, and neck.

Tips for Keeping It Healthy

▶ Express yourself truthfully. Speak your truth in any way that works for you, whether through writing, singing, or talking.

▶ Channel Reiki or healing energy to your throat chakra.

▶ Work with blue crystals such as sodalite or celestite.

▶ Visualize a blue wheel of light spinning in your throat chakra, and imagine bright white light passing easily through the spinning chakra.

▶ Enjoy blue foods such as blueberries and blackberries, and foods that soothe your throat, such as honey or chamomile tea.

▶ In yoga, vocalize mantras such as Om to open throat chakra energy.

▶ Diffuse essential oils that support the throat chakra, such as chamomile or peppermint.

Third Eye Chakra · Ajna

LOCATION: Center of your forehead

COLOR: Violet

Your third eye chakra—also known as the sixth chakra or by its Sanskrit name Ajna—is located in the center of your forehead. This is the energetic center of reason, intellect, intuition, and spiritual guidance. When this chakra is out of balance, you may overthink things or have disturbed dreams or sleep. Physically, imbalances may manifest in headaches, mind fog, and eye and sinus issues.

Tips for Keeping It Healthy

▸ Meditate. Meditation is an activity that helps you connect with your third eye chakra and with higher guidance.

▸ Channel Reiki or healing energy to your third eye chakra.

▸ Pay attention to flashes of insight and dreams, which are your higher guidance trying to communicate with you through your third eye chakra.

▸ Work with violet or purple crystals such as charoite and amethyst.

▸ Visualize a violet wheel of light spinning in your third eye chakra, and imagine a bright white light passing easily through the spinning chakra.

▸ Purple foods such as eggplant, purple yams, and purple cabbage can help balance the energy of this chakra.

▸ In yoga, practice breathing techniques such as alternate nostril breathing to activate this chakra.

▸ Diffuse essential oils to support the third eye energy, such as lavender.

Crown Chakra · Sahasrara

LOCATION: About an inch above the top of your head

COLOR: White

Your crown chakra—also known as the seventh chakra or by its Sanskrit name Sahasrara—is located just above the crown of your head. This is the energetic center that connects you to a higher power and your higher self. When this chakra is out of balance, you may struggle with spiritual issues or feel a disconnection from the universe. Physically, imbalances may manifest as systemic issues such as fibromyalgia, as well as issues of the bones and skin.

Tips for Keeping It Healthy

▶ Meditation or prayer is essential for connecting and maintaining active crown chakra energy.

▶ Channel Reiki or healing energy to your crown chakra.

▶ Work with clear or white crystals such as clear quartz or howlite.

▶ Visualize a white wheel of light spinning in your crown chakra, and imagine bright white light passing easily through the spinning chakra.

▶ Brief fasting and clear liquids such as water or coconut water can support the energy of this chakra as well.

▶ In yoga, sitting with hands in prayer position while chanting Om can help activate this chakra and keep it balanced.

▶ Diffuse essential oils that support the crown chakra, such as sandalwood or jasmine.

The Hara Line Chakras

These seven chakras make up the hara line chakras. The hara line flows through these chakras and connects you to the energy of the Earth (through your feet) and the energy of the cosmos (through your crown). During a Reiki attunement, the Reiki Master-Teacher connects the Reiki energy to each of these chakras to allow you to serve as a conduit for the energy.

It is essential for energy to connect to and flow through each chakra to maintain balance. Imbalances can be related to a single chakra, as noted in the previous sections, or to the interaction between a few chakras. For instance, if you get plenty of creative ideas (which are born in the sacral chakra), but you have trouble with creative expression (which arises in the throat chakra), there may be a disconnect between these two chakras and working with both to provide balance can help.

As another example, autoimmune disease itself is generated in the root chakra, but its symptoms often manifest in a different chakra. For example, Hashimoto's thyroiditis is an autoimmune condition that manifests in the throat (thyroid) region and affects both the root and throat chakras. Therefore, seeking to balance and connect these two chakras can help when you work with this condition.

Methods to Balance the Hara Line Chakras

▶ To connect chakras using Reiki, you can hold your hands in a bridge position (one hand on one chakra, the other on another) and visualize the Reiki energy running between the two chakras.

▶ To connect the hara line chakras all together with Source and Earth energy, visualize an energy shower. Imagine you are standing under a waterfall of white light. See the light flowing down from the waterfall, in through your crown chakra, down the hara line through each chakra, and then out of your feet and into the Earth.

▶ You can also connect the hara line chakras from the Earth up. Visualize white light coming from the Earth, up through the bottoms of your feet, flowing through all your chakras along the hara line, and then coming out your crown chakra and connecting you to the energy of the cosmos.

Other Chakras

The chakras of your hara line are your major chakras, but you also have minor chakras. Minor chakras exist in each of the following locations:

▸ Ears (linked to heart chakra)

▸ Sides of rib cage (intercostals, linked to heart chakra)

▸ Shoulders (linked to throat chakra)

▸ Elbows (linked to root chakra)

▸ Knees (linked to root chakra)

▸ Clavicles (linked to third eye chakra)

▸ Either side of groin (linked to third eye chakra)

▸ Either side of belly button (linked to throat chakra)

▸ Hands (linked to crown chakra)

▸ Feet (linked to crown chakra)

Complementary Practices and Tools

Reiki works wonderfully well as a modality by itself, but it is also a great tool to combine with other practices. I seldom practice Reiki in a vacuum. Depending on the needs of my healing partner, I may weave in a number of other complementary practices that help direct and support the Reiki energy.

It's important to understand that each of these practices deals with the same substance—vibrating universal energy—but different modalities may be appropriate for different healing partners. I rely largely on my intuition to determine which of these practices to use, although if a healing partner requests a specific complementary practice, I make it a point to work with that modality during their sessions as well.

Meditation

Whether using guided meditation, visualization, affirmation, or mindfulness, meditation is a wonderful complement to Reiki healing. Meditation is simply allowing a state of mindfulness. It can be as easy as sitting and focusing on breathing, or it can be something more complex. Prayer is a form of meditation, as is reciting affirmations or visualizing. All allow your healing partner to become an active participant in the process of their healing through their own intention.

Crystals

I adore working with crystals and gemstones. The different colors and structures of the crystals cause them to vibrate at various energetic frequencies to support different types of healing. Although there's a lot to learn about crystals, a simple guideline is to work with crystals that match the color of the chakra you are balancing. For example, if you're working on heart chakra energy, you may wish to place pink or green healing crystals on the heart chakra and channel Reiki to your healing partner right through the crystals.

Sound Healing and Music

Sound has its own vibration and frequency, and it is a great way to help balance energy. I like to work with singing bowls or recorded music called solfeggio—a specific tone-based audio file connected to each chakra—that supports the energy of each chakra, but you can also use mantras, chanting, singing, or even simple meditative music to help create a vibrational space conducive to healing during your Reiki sessions.

Plant Medicine

Plants are living beings with their own vibrational frequency. You can have live plants present in a session to contribute to the vibrational atmosphere of the space, or suggest your healing partners work with the energy of certain plants (such as through teas or in bath water). Plants allow your healing partners to actively participate in their own energy healing process by working with plant energy. Please note that as a Reiki healing practitioner, you are not allowed to prescribe, so be very careful about the plants you suggest your healing partners take orally. Instead, recommend working with plants through activities such as burning herbs or soaking in a bath with them.

Traditional Chinese Medicine

Traditional Chinese Medicine (TCM) works with balancing the yin and yang energy (positive and negative polarity) in the body. And though you need to avoid prescribing substances unless you're a doctor, you can certainly work with other aspects of TCM to balance elemental energies of earth, wood, fire, water, and metal by balancing the flow of chi energy with movement and feng shui practices.

Ayurveda

Ayurveda is another system that works with creating balance of the different types of elemental energies—earth, air, fire, water, and space—through energy healing practices. Again, although you cannot prescribe substances unless you are an Ayurvedic doctor, you can help your healing partners participate in their own energy healing by engaging in personal practices involving food or movement to bring elemental energy balance.

Aroma and Color Therapy

Aromatherapy and color therapy can also help create energetic balance because different aromas and colors vibrate at different frequencies. Diffusing essential oils is a great way to bring aromatherapy into your sessions, and using various colored lights can also help balance the energy of the chakras.

Acupuncture and Acupressure

Acupuncture and acupressure create energetic balance by ensuring energy is flowing correctly through the meridian system. These work quite well as complementary therapies to Reiki if you are certified to use them. The Emotional Freedom Technique (EFT), or tapping, is a simple acupressure method that is helpful for creating balance, and it allows your healing partner to play an active role in their healing.

Other Energy Healing Modalities

Other energy healing modalities may be appropriate as well. For example, I love to work with polarity therapy with my healing partners, which is a method for creating balance of the elemental energies of earth, air, fire, water, and ether. Reiki also works well with neurolinguistic programming (NLP), massage therapy, Quantum Touch, Healing Touch, and many other energy healing modalities that support the greatest good of your healing partners.

CHAPTER TWO

First Degree Reiki Training

First Degree Reiki is what I like to refer to as "hands-on" or "friends and family" Reiki. It is a great first step on your Reiki journey because it allows you to learn the basics of Reiki energy and experience how it manifests in both your own energy field and in the energetics of your healing partners. As an attuned First Degree Reiki practitioner, you'll be able to channel First Degree Reiki energy through your hands so your healing partner can draw the energy in. In this chapter, you'll learn the information First Degree Reiki practitioners need to know and understand to practice First Degree Reiki and lay the foundation for practicing additional degrees of Reiki.

Five Principles of Reiki

Usui Sensei taught all his students the five principles of Reiki, which are simple ideals that all Reiki practitioners must strive to attain. They deal with attitudes and beliefs that support the flow of Reiki energy in a way that serves the greatest good of the practitioner and their healing partners. Each of the principles focuses on living and being in the moment by starting with the words "Just for today." This phrase is extremely important, and it reminds Reiki practitioners to focus on the now and do the best they can in any moment.

Usui Sensei recommended reflecting on these principles in meditation. I suggest finding ways to incorporate them into your life in ways that best serve you. Personally, I reflect on the principles when I wake each morning and before I go to sleep each night, as well as before I channel Reiki. The five principles are as follows.

Just for today, I will not worry.

Worry and fear keep us from working from a place of love, which is where Reiki energy originates. And Usui Sensei reminds you in this principle that you do the best you can from moment to moment. If you catch yourself worrying, then you have slipped out of present-time focus and into future projection. With this principle, you can remember to bring yourself back into the Eternal Moment of Now, which is a focus on the present time that allows you to slip into a state of *being* instead of *doing*.

Just for today, I will not anger.

Just as worry brings us out of love and present-time focus into future projection, anger brings us out of love and present-time focus into projection in the past. When we are angry at someone, it is because of something that was said or done in a past moment, and anger causes us to dwell on the past instead of focusing on the present.

Just for today, I will be kind to all living creatures.

Kindness is at the heart of Reiki, which seeks to share loving energy from a place of compassion and giving. This principle reminds us of the compassionate and giving mindset from which Reiki is best able to flow.

Just for today, I will do my work with truth and integrity.

Reiki is a pure form of energy that arises from ultimate truth. And though anyone attuned can channel Reiki energy, the ability to share and channel this energy requires a great deal of personal integrity. This principle reminds you to step into a place of truth as you share Reiki energy with the intention of serving the greatest good.

Just for today, I will be grateful.

As part of my Reiki practice, I always express gratitude for the ability to channel this beautiful energy. Gratitude is a principle that is interwoven throughout the practice of Reiki because it reminds us that the energy doesn't come *from* us, but rather flows *through* us—we are merely conduits for universal energy to serve the greatest good of both the practitioner and healing partner.

Gassho Meditation

Dr. Usui also taught a simple form of meditation for all Reiki practitioners that he called *Gassho*. Gassho meditation is important for Reiki practitioners because it helps bring you into the present moment and settle into the Reiki energy before you begin to channel it to another. Usui Sensei recommended practicing Gassho (or another form of meditation) daily, as well as for a few moments at the beginning of a Reiki session to invite Reiki energy to flow.

To perform Gassho:

1. Place your hands in prayer position in front of your heart.

2. Breathe naturally, focusing on the place where the tips of your middle fingers intersect.

3. If your mind starts to wander, gently return your attention to the intersection of your middle fingers.

4. If doing this before a Reiki session, ask for the Reiki energy to flow. When you feel it begin to flow in your hands, begin your Reiki session.

5. Do this (or another form of meditation) for 10 to 20 minutes every day.

Three Reiki Degrees

In Usui Ryoho Reiki, there are three degrees to which practitioners can be attuned. Different Reiki Master-Teachers may teach and attune the degrees in various configurations, with differing recommended times between each degree, but the principles, energetic attunement, and responsibilities of the Reiki practitioner are standardized for each degree. Some people who are seeking to learn Reiki mostly for personal growth often choose to stop at First Degree Reiki. Practitioners who wish to practice Reiki professionally or as part of another healing practice may choose to learn First Degree and Second Degree Reiki. Those who wish to teach and attune others to Reiki will go on to earn their Reiki Master-Teacher Degree.

First Degree Reiki (Shoden)

First Degree Reiki is hands-on Reiki. Practitioners attuned to this degree of Reiki are able to place their hands on their healing partner (or hover them a few inches above their healing partner's body) and channel Reiki in-person to that healing partner. All Reiki practitioners must be attuned to First Degree Reiki and, as with all degrees of Reiki, you must be attuned by a Reiki Master-Teacher. Your instructor will also teach you the following in this degree:

◆ The history of Reiki
◆ Your Reiki lineage extending back through Dr. Usui
◆ Hand positions for healing self
◆ Hand positions for healing others
◆ The five principles of Reiki

If you are learning Reiki for personal reasons or to work only with self-healing, friends and family, and pets, then you may wish to complete your Reiki journey here, as this will provide you with everything you need to know to incorporate Reiki practices into your personal life.

Second Degree Reiki (Okuden)

In Second Degree Reiki, you will be attuned so you can channel a stronger Reiki energy. You must be attuned to First Degree Reiki before you can be attuned to Second Degree. During this degree, you will learn symbols and processes so you can channel Reiki at a distance across both time and space. Second Degree Reiki builds on what you learned in First Degree Reiki, and it is strongly recommended that if you wish to practice Reiki professionally, or as part of another professional healing practice you engage in, you learn and are attuned to Second Degree Reiki. In Second Degree Reiki, you will learn:

◆ The three pillars of Reiki
◆ The three symbols of Second Degree Reiki and their uses

- How to work intuitively in a Reiki session
- How to channel Reiki across a distance of time or space

Additionally, your Reiki Master-Teacher may also offer some of the following curriculum:

- Best practices for setting up a Reiki practice
- More in-depth information about subtle anatomy
- Business information about setting up a practice, such as required paperwork, insurance, and licensing requirements in your state
- Nontraditional Reiki symbols and their uses
- How to set up a distance Reiki healing room
- How to work with your Reiki guides

Reiki Master-Teacher Degree (Shinpiden)

In Usui Ryoho Reiki, this is the final degree of Reiki that practitioners can achieve. Some other forms of Reiki may expand upon this information, but traditional Usui Ryoho Reiki ends its formal training in this degree.

You must first be attuned to First Degree and Second Degree Reiki before you can be attuned to Master-Teacher energy. You should consider attunement to the Reiki Master-Teacher Degree if you wish to teach and attune others to Reiki, or if you'd simply like to carry your Usui Ryoho Reiki training to its ultimate conclusion. In this degree, you will be attuned to Master-Teacher Reiki energy and will also learn about the following:

- How to draw and use the Reiki Master symbol
- How to develop your Reiki curriculum for each level and what information it should contain
- Procedures and processes for attuning others to all degrees of Reiki both in-person and at a distance
- Ethics for practicing and teaching Reiki

Anyone can attain and be attuned to any of the degrees of Reiki; no special talents are required. Instead, if you are called on the Reiki journey, listen to the guidance of your soul. Because you have been drawn to Reiki, you are meant to channel its energy.

Reiki Attunements

To channel Reiki energy, a Reiki Master-Teacher must attune you to that degree of Reiki energy. Once you are attuned to a certain degree of Reiki energy, you will be for life. You will never need to be reattuned to the same degree of Reiki energy again.

So, what is an attunement? In an attunement, a Reiki Master-Teacher aligns your vibrational energy with the energetic frequency of the degree of Reiki energy you will be channeling. I look at the alignment as removing a filter or flipping a switch in the practitioner to allow that degree of Reiki energy to flow in an unrestricted manner. Attunements only take a few minutes, but they create a profound change in the Reiki practitioner due to changes in your personal frequency and vibration.

Because your energetic frequency changes with each successive attunement to higher degrees of Reiki, I recommend leaving at least 21 days between attunements (the amount of time Usui Sensei fasted and meditated on Mount Kurama) to become fully accustomed to the vibrational changes that have occurred.

Attunements can occur either in-person or at a distance. I prefer in-person attunements so my students have the opportunity to practice under my supervision after attunement, but that isn't always possible. I have attuned many people using both methods (in-person and distance), and both methods have always resulted in the person receiving the attunement aligning with the degree of Reiki energy they are now able to channel.

What to Expect

Your First Degree Reiki attunement will take just a few minutes; it may be longer if you are part of a group of people being attuned. During the attunement, you will sit with your eyes closed and your hands in Gassho. Although different Reiki Master-Teachers follow different processes for attunement, most will likely have the following elements:

1. At the start of the attunement, the Reiki Master-Teacher will ask you to silently affirm your desire and consent to be attuned to First Degree Reiki energy.

2. While you sit with your eyes closed, you may hear or sense the Reiki Master-Teacher moving around you. (When I am attuning groups, I always

gently touch the shoulder of the person I am attuning so they know it is their turn.) Breathe deeply and allow any sensations you notice during the attunement.

3. During the attunement, the Reiki Master-Teacher will use Reiki symbols to align your energetic system, including your hara line chakras, with First Degree Reiki energy.

4. At the end of the attunement, the Reiki Master-Teacher will give thanks to Reiki and to Reiki Masters past, present, and future for your attunement, affirming that you will move forward as a powerful and confident First Degree Reiki practitioner.

5. The Reiki Master-Teacher may also ask you to take a moment to reflect in gratitude and to affirm your willingness to move forward as a powerful and confident First Degree Reiki practitioner.

Possible Reactions

You may experience some reactions during or immediately following your attunement, or you may not experience anything—all reactions are natural. The following are possible reactions to your attunement:

◆ You may experience a deep sense of peace or relaxation.
◆ You may have visions or notice swirling colors behind your eyes.
◆ You may feel an emotional release or feel rapidly shifting emotions.
◆ You may experience a profound sense of joy.
◆ You may notice warmth or tingling in your hands and chakras.
◆ You may notice a slight, allover buzzing in your body.
◆ You may notice no changes at all.

You may also experience a vibrational shift as you align with the First Degree Reiki energy in the period following your First Degree attunement. This can cause mild symptoms as your body adapts to the new frequency, or it may not cause any issues at all. Again, all reactions are natural.

During this period, you are encouraged to care deeply for yourself. Channel Reiki to yourself daily by using the hand positions you will be provided for self-care, or by channeling small amounts of Reiki to yourself when you have time, such as while you're watching television, meditating, or drifting off to sleep. During this 21-day period, you should also drink plenty of water and seek to move and eat in ways that nurture your good health. You will be able to channel First Degree Reiki energy to yourself and others immediately following your attunement.

Some reactions people have noticed following their First Degree Reiki attunement include the following:

◆ You may notice ongoing warmth or tingling in your hands, or you may notice that your hands "turn on" at certain times. If your hands turn on, either ground the energy by touching the ground or channel the Reiki to yourself.

◆ You may be a bit more emotional than usual. Be gentle with yourself and allow these emotions.

◆ You may experience mild physical symptoms, such as a stuffy nose or mild sleep disturbances. These will generally go away on their own as your body adapts to the energy.

◆ You may notice you have more intense dreams than you have had in the past. This is often guidance from your higher self or spirit guides, so see if you can discover what your dreams mean using a dream analysis dictionary.

◆ You may notice you are feeling more intuitive in general. Try to listen to your intuition and act upon it.

The Mechanics of Reiki Healing

So how, exactly, does First Degree Reiki work, and what will you or your healing partners notice? Although the experience is different for everyone, there are some generalizations we can make to help you and your healing partners better understand the process. With your deeper understanding, you can also better explain the process to your healing partners before and after their Reiki sessions.

How Reiki Flows

First Degree Reiki is universal energy that comes from the Source (what others may refer to as the Universe, the Zero Point Field, or God). Your First Degree attunement has aligned you to this universal energy so that it can flow from the universe, through you, and out of you through your hands, auric field, gaze, or breath. From there, your healing partner draws the Reiki energy into their energetic field and body.

The Reiki energy is all around you. You can draw it into you through your breath, pull it from the Earth through your feet, feel it entering through your skin from all around you, or visualize it flowing from the universe in through your crown chakra and out through your gaze, breath, auric field, and/or hands.

Reiki energy is intelligent energy. It always flows in ways that serve the greatest good of both the Reiki practitioner and the healing partner, and it is never harmful or dangerous. Because this universal energy is so intelligent, Reiki will always flow where it's needed. This means that if someone has a headache, you could put your hands on their foot to help with the headache, and the energy would naturally flow there. However, I'm a big fan of meeting your healing partners right where they are. If you told me you had a headache and I put my hand on your foot, you might not feel heard. Therefore, I'd likely place my hands on your head, both because the energy can get their more quickly and directly, and because I want you as my healing partner to feel validated and heard in what you have told me.

Although your hands are the most common means of delivering Reiki energy, you can also direct it through your gaze, by beaming it from your auric field, or even through your breath. You may wish to use a combination of all these techniques during your Reiki sessions, although channeling it through the hands is the most common way First Degree Reiki practitioners deliver the energy.

Turning Reiki On and Off

Most First Degree Reiki practitioners can feel the flow of Reiki as warmth, tingling, pushing, pulling, or other changes of sensation in their hands. Likewise, your healing partner will often experience the drawing in of Reiki as warmth, relaxation, tingling, or other changes of sensation in the area where the Reiki is being channeled.

Intention is your main tool to "turn on" Reiki. Although it can, and does, turn on spontaneously from time to time, when you are working in a Reiki healing session, you simply ask to have the Reiki flow. I suggest doing this by starting every Reiki session with your hands in Gassho and asking for the Reiki energy to move through you. After a session, you can "turn off" the Reiki by grounding the energy and breaking the energetic link between you and your healing partner. To ground the energy, place your hands on the ground. To break the energetic link, run your hands under cool or cold water. Grounding and breaking the energetic link is an important step, and one you should do at the end of every Reiki session.

Typical Healing Sessions

You will develop your own practices and be guided by each individual healing partner, and it is helpful to first understand a typical Reiki healing session. By working within the structure of a healing session, you can then begin to add your own touches based on intuitive information you receive about each of your healing partners during a session. However, even if you don't receive any intuitive information during a session, you can follow the basic session structure and still provide a complete Reiki treatment that serves the greatest good for your healing partner. Having a basic structure for a session provides the form that then allows you the freedom to act on intuitive information if you receive it.

Preparing for a Session

I always take about 10 minutes before my healing partner arrives to prepare for a session. This allows me to get into the meditative and energetic space where I can listen to my intuition and work with it in ways that serve my healing partner's greatest good. Before your healing partner arrives, take five to ten minutes to meditate or sit with your hands in Gassho. During this time, you can express gratitude to Reiki, ask the energy to flow, and ask to receive any intuitive information that may help you as you work with your healing partner. Additionally, you may wish to ensure any necessary objects are available and any environmental settings are prepared.

SELF-TREATMENT

To prepare for and perform a self-treatment:

1. Find a place where the session won't be disturbed.

2. Adjust the environment for comfort by ensuring the lighting is soft, the temperature is comfortable, and the space allows you to sit or lie comfortably during your self-treatment.

3. Sit with your hands in Gassho and ask for the Reiki to flow.

4. When you feel the Reiki flow, use the self-treatment hand positions (beginning on page 47), holding your hands in each position for three to five minutes. You can use a Reiki timer to do this—there are many Reiki timer apps as well as YouTube videos that play music with a discreet chime when it's time to switch hand positions. If you feel intuitively guided for alternative placements, listen to this guidance and move your hands as guided. If the guidance stops, return to the basic hand positions.

5. At the end of treatment, return your hands to Gassho and offer thanks to the Reiki energy for flowing in ways that serve your greatest good.

6. Run your hands under cold water to ground yourself and shut off the flow of Reiki energy.

TREATING A HEALING PARTNER

Your healing partner can be fully clothed during a treatment. I typically ask healing partners to remove their shoes and cellphones, and I remove mine as well so I can be grounded during a session. I also ask that they remove their watches and glasses, if they wear them. Remove any jewelry you're wearing that may get in the way—jingly bracelets, long pendants that can bump them on the head, etc. Ask your healing partner to tell you if there is anything you can supply to make them more comfortable.

To perform a treatment for a healing partner:

1. Set up in a place where the session won't be disturbed. If possible, use a massage table for treatment. Alternatively, you can have your healing partner sit in a chair that you can move around easily. Clean the table or chair.

2. Adjust the environment for comfort by ensuring the lighting is soft and the temperature is comfortable. Add other things conducive to a good atmosphere, such as diffusing essential oils.

3. Have a light blanket, pillows, bolsters, tissues, and a glass of water available.

4. Have your healing partner fill out any necessary paperwork and conduct a brief consultation. Ask why your healing partner is seeking Reiki and explain what they might experience during the session.

5. Ask for permission to touch. If you don't receive permission, during the session you can hover your hands a few inches above your healing partner's body.

6. Have your healing partner stand in front of you. Sweep their aura by running your hand a few inches away from their body down through their auric field along the front, sides, and back. At the end of each sweep, flick excess energy into the ground from your fingers. The Earth will neutralize the energy.

7. Have your healing partner lie on the table on their back with their arms and legs uncrossed or sit in a chair.

8. Stand in Gassho for a moment until you feel the Reiki energy flow.

9. Place your hands on your healing partner's shoulders and stand that way for a few moments to allow you to get used to one another's energy. Watch your healing partner for a subtle sign of release, such as a sigh or a shift in position, signaling they are ready for the session to begin.

10. Conduct a Reiki session using the hand positions beginning on page 62. Hold each hand position for three to five minutes using a Reiki music timer. If you feel intuitively guided during the session, move your hands as your intuition directs. Always keep your eyes open during the session so you can observe your healing partner's reactions.

11. Upon completing the session, give thanks to Reiki and affirm that the Reiki energy serves your healing partner's greatest good.

Ending a Session

At the conclusion of the session, have your healing partner sit up on the table or, if seated, open their eyes.

1. Sweep their aura again, touching the ground at the bottom of each sweep.

2. Give your healing partner a glass of cool water to ground them and step out to run your hands under cold water to break the energetic connection between the two of you.

3. After the session, allow your healing partner to ask questions or share any experiences they wish to with you.

Range of Results

Your healing partner may experience a range of results. It's always best to suggest they drink plenty of water throughout the remainder of the day, as water can flush out any toxins that have been released into the body as a result of the vibrational shift that occurred during the Reiki session.

All experiences that result from a Reiki session exist to serve the greatest good of your healing partner. Some things your healing partners might experience include:

◆ Emotional release, rapid emotional shifts, or slight emotional shifts as a result of vibrational change
◆ A brief uptick in symptoms followed by a lessening of symptoms, or sometimes just a lessening of symptoms
◆ Increased intuition
◆ Increased spiritual awareness
◆ Vivid dreams
◆ Deeper sleep or mild sleep disturbances
◆ A sense of relaxation or deep peace
◆ Sleepiness
◆ Increased energy
◆ A "buzzing" feeling throughout the body
◆ Sensations of warmth
◆ No noticeable results

All these results are normal, as each individual will receive what they need from the Reiki session. In general, I explain the possible experiences after a Reiki session and invite them to reach out to me if they need help or assurance. In general, most of these effects will be mild.

Receiving Reiki

The best way to understand what it feels like to receive Reiki is to work with another Reiki practitioner or to channel Reiki to yourself if you're a newly attuned practitioner. However, it's always helpful to understand the range of experiences people might have during a Reiki session in order to explain to your healing partners what they might experience while they're on your table.

Who or What Can Receive Reiki?

Because everything is made up of the same energy that simply takes different forms, anything or anyone can receive Reiki. Here are some examples:

- Friends and family
- Clients/healing partners
- Plants and/or the water/food you give your plants
- Electronics
- Cars and public transportation
- Crystals
- Your home and the spaces where you live, work, and play
- Pets
- Food and beverages
- Bathwater
- Jewelry
- Gifts
- Clothing and shoes
- Paper (with your affirmations written on them)

  There are also a few people you should not channel Reiki to:

- Anyone who tells you they don't wish to receive it
- People who have a pacemaker (it can affect the energy)
- Anyone whose medical doctor has told them they shouldn't receive energy healing

Getting Ready

Before a healing partner receives Reiki, they may wish to do the following:

- Eat healthy foods and drink plenty of water for 24 to 48 hours before the treatment.
- Engage in gentle but not overly strenuous movement.
- Ask that the Reiki serve their highest good.
- Avoid alcohol and intoxicants for 24 to 48 hours before a treatment.

Sensing Energy

During a treatment, you may sense the energy of your healing partner, and your healing partner may sense energy from you or from the Reiki.

SENSING ENERGY AS A PRACTITIONER

As a practitioner, you may sense energy in various ways:

◆ You may notice changes in sensation in the palms of your hands, such as increased or decreased temperature, tingling, pushing, pulling, or prickling.

◆ You might see colors or wavy energy patterns where energy is needed.

◆ You might suddenly be aware of changes in energy as a "knowing."

◆ You may "hear" voices or words as persistent thoughts in your head.

◆ You might notice sensations in your body directing you to where your healing partner needs the energy.

◆ You may notice differences in pressure such as increased ear or sinus pressure or similar sensations.

◆ You may "see" images in your mind's eye that direct your treatment.

◆ You may sense a release of energy as a "whoosh" or rushing sensation.

SENSING ENERGY AS A HEALING PARTNER

Your healing partner may also notice shifts in energy. This may manifest in various ways such as:

◆ They may experience rapid or mild emotional shifts, or have an emotional release.

◆ They might see colors or images in their mind's eye.

◆ They may notice warmth, coolness, or tingling sensations in their body.

◆ They may feel peaceful and relaxed or slightly "buzzy."

◆ They may experience a "whoosh" or rushing sensation either physically or emotionally.

Aftercare

After a session, I try to talk minimally to my healing partners because I want them to have as much space as they need to experience anything that arises as the result of energetic shifts. However, I do typically ask if they have questions. Additionally, I advise my healing partners to:

◆ Drink lots of water.

◆ Avoid alcohol or intoxicants for 24 hours.

◆ Go home and take a warm bath with sea salt or Himalayan pink salt in the water.

◆ Eat light, nourishing food for the next few meals.

◆ Meditate for 10 to 15 minutes.

◆ Try to get a good night's sleep.

◆ Keep a journal to record feelings, insights, or dreams that arise.

Managing Your Energy

I find that many people drawn to the energy healing arts have a deeply empathic nature. And with that deep compassion and empathy comes a desire to help their healing partners feel better, regardless of the energetic cost to themselves as the practitioner. Managing your own energy is essential to your well-being during Reiki treatments because you don't want to make your healing partner feel better while you feel worse. The goal is for you both to leave the session vibrating at a higher frequency.

Reiki energy comes *through* you and not *from* you, so in an ideal world, there shouldn't be a transfer of your personal energy to your healing partner. However, in many cases, especially when the Reiki practitioner is empathic, such a transfer occurs anyway unless you engage in deliberate practices to manage your own energy. Grounding and clearing practices can help you maintain good energy hygiene (keeping your own energy clear and protected) before, during, and after a Reiki session.

Basic Grounding Practices

Grounding is essential before, during, and after a session because it helps you maintain your own energetic boundaries so you're not giving away your energy to another or depleting your personal energy.

- Always work with your feet flat on the floor. If it's feasible, have your feet bare during the session.
- After the session, run your hands under cool or cold water to ground you and break the energetic connection to your healing partner. Ground your healing partner by sweeping their aura, ensuring you finish by touching the ground, and offering them a glass of cool water.
- After your healing partner leaves, sit or stand with your feet flat on the floor and visualize roots growing from your feet and extending deep into the Earth.

Basic Clearing Practices

Clearing is essential before, during, and after a session as well.

- Before and after a session, clear the healing space by burning sage, incense, or palo santo; striking a singing bowl; or visualizing white light filling the room.
- During the session, if you receive intuitive information—especially as sensations in your body—act on the information, thank the universe for providing it, and then flush it by visualizing white light coming down through your crown, through your body, and pushing the information or sensation out through your feet and into the Earth.
- After the session, take a "Reiki shower" by visualizing Reiki energy as a waterfall above you. Step into the Reiki energy and allow it to flush throughout your body and flow from the bottoms of your feet into the Earth.

Maintaining a Healthy Reiki Practice

Maintaining a healthy Reiki practice means using energy hygiene and practices that create a safe space for your healing partner as well as an energetically sound space for yourself. A healthy Reiki practice looks out for your physical, emotional, and spiritual health with the following methods:

- Maintain healthy boundaries with your healing partners.
- Always ground and clear energy before and after every session.
- Practice self-Reiki and Gassho or meditation for at least five minutes every day.
- Intend for your Reiki to always serve the greatest good for you and your healing partners.
- Set aside expectations for you or your healing partners. Instead, enter each Reiki session in the spirit of "allowing" and let the Reiki energy guide you throughout the session.
- Focus on the Reiki principles.
- Always express gratitude for the Reiki energy.
- Seek to learn as much as you can about Reiki and energy healing through continuing education.

CHAPTER THREE

First Degree Reiki Healing Techniques

Now that you've learned the background information essential for practicing First Degree Reiki, it's time to get into the details. One of the things I love about First Degree Reiki is that it provides a complete, structured system of techniques that serves as a step-by-step plan for a Reiki session. With the information in the previous chapter, the techniques in this chapter, and attunement from a Reiki Master-Teacher, you'll be ready to start providing hands-on Reiki to yourself and others as soon as you are attuned.

Methods to Share First Degree Reiki

First Degree Usui Ryoho Reiki is primarily a hands-on form in which you provide Reiki energy in-person by placing your hands on your healing partners in different hand positions. However, touch may not be feasible or comfortable for some practitioners and healing partners for various reasons, so First Degree Reiki offers other ways of delivering the energy to in-person healing partners. At the beginning of every in-person Reiki session, ask for permission to touch and then respond within the session according to your healing partner's wishes. In some cases, licensing requirements in your state may prohibit touch as a professional practice unless you have a "license to touch" (often, a massage therapy license), so it's important that if you are practicing Reiki professionally, you do so in accordance with your state's laws and licensing requirements.

Hands-On

In hands-on Reiki healing, place your hands directly on your healing partner (or yourself) using direct touch. This is the best method to use if your healing partner gives permission for touch, as many people don't have much loving touch in their lives and Reiki is a way to provide it. Hands-on Reiki also generates a gentle, healing warmth that is calming and relaxing. You can use the Reiki hand positions (page 47) or place your hands intuitively depending on what you feel guided to do.

Hovering

If you don't receive permission to touch, or you don't have a license to touch when you're practicing professionally, hover your hands between one and four inches above your healing partner's body using the Reiki hand positions or hand positions you are intuitively guided to take. Although this isn't as intimate as hands-on touch, in some cases it may feel safer or more comfortable for your healing partner.

Directing Reiki with Your Gaze

You can also direct Reiki with your gaze by standing near your healing partner and gazing softly at the place where you would typically place your hands. Visualize the Reiki energy coming down through the crown of your head and flowing through your eyes and into your healing partner. You need to be in the presence of your healing partner to do this.

Intuitive Healing

Even though First Degree Usui Ryoho Reiki provides a system of hand positions, I always encourage my students to work with their intuition as much as possible during a Reiki session. If you feel intuitively guided to place your hands in a certain spot, listen to that guidance. Your intuition exists to guide you as a Reiki practitioner. Following this guidance can help direct the Reiki energy quickly and efficiently to where it is most needed.

I understand that it can be difficult or stressful to rely on intuition during a Reiki healing session with a healing partner, particularly when you're new to the practice, but it doesn't have to be. It's actually simple: If you're guided to place your hands somewhere, follow that guidance. When you feel guided to move your hands to a different location, move them there. If you don't notice any intuitive guidance, follow the system of hand positions, always allowing room for guidance to arise throughout a session.

If you'd like to try working with intuition in a session, ask for intuitive guidance at the start of the session. Stand at your healing partner's head with your hands in Gassho, holding your fingertips in front of your third eye chakra. Then, ask to be guided during your session. Once you feel guidance, move your hands to where you feel you should place them. If you don't notice any guidance, start with the hand positions, holding space for the possibility of guidance during a session.

Guidance may arise in the following ways:

◆ The desire to move or place your hands in a certain location
◆ A "knowing" that you should place your hands there
◆ Visual signals such as the appearance of wavy lines (similar to heat waves) or color inlays over a certain part of the body
◆ Signals such as words appearing in your mind (or being heard with your ears), like "left arm" or "head"
◆ Pain in various areas of your body that you know aren't related to anything physically happening with you (for example, if you experience a shoulder pain and you know nothing is wrong with your shoulder, it may be your intuition telling you to place your hands on your healing partner's shoulder)

Hand Positions for Self-Healing

Self-healing is extremely important for Reiki practitioners of all degrees. I channel Reiki to myself daily—even if it's only for five minutes—and I also receive Reiki (hands-on or at a distance) from many of my friends who are Reiki practitioners themselves. Even if it's for only five minutes a day, channeling self-Reiki can help you feel invigorated, maintain energetic balance throughout your subtle anatomy, and help you work through any mental, physical, spiritual, or emotional dis-ease you may encounter. Practice a full hands-on self-Reiki treatment, using intuition or the hand positions that follow, daily for 21 days after each Reiki attunement or when you are ill.

When using the Reiki hand positions for yourself or others:

◆ Use a light touch—don't press too hard or rest the weight of your hands and arms on yourself or your healing partner.

◆ Cup your hands lightly with your fingers lightly pressed together and your thumbs tucked into the sides of your palms as illustrated, unless otherwise indicated.

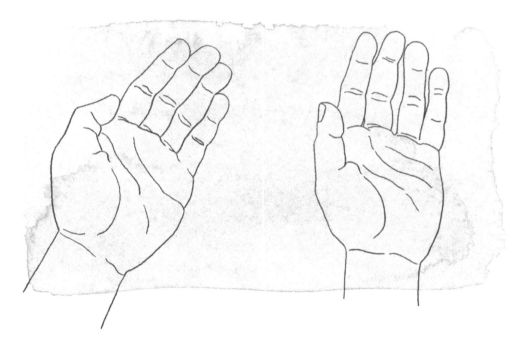

◆ Hold each hand **position for three** to five minutes, or until you are guided to move your hands.

◆ If any hand position is uncomfortable for you, adapt it so you are able to hold the position comfortably for three to five minutes.

◆ For self-Reiki, either lie on your back in a comfortable position or sit upright in a chair with your feet resting flat on the floor.

Eyes

This hand position channels Reiki to your third eye and crown chakras, as well as to your eyes, brain, forehead, and sinuses.

1. With your hands cupped and thumbs tucked into the sides of your hand, lightly rest the heels of your palms on your cheekbones.

2. Rest your fingertips lightly on your forehead at your hairline.

Cheeks

This hand position channels Reiki to your crown and third eye chakras, as well as to your cheeks, ears, and jaw.

1. Lightly hook your thumbs behind each ear.

2. Rest the pinky side of your cupped hands along your jaw, outer eyes, and eyebrows.

3. Rest your fingers lightly on your temples.

Back of Head

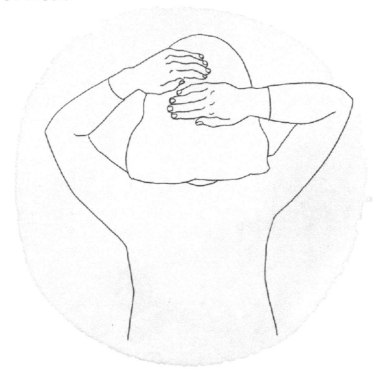

This hand position channels Reiki to your brain, pineal gland, skull, and the upper vertebrae of your neck. Some people may find this hand position needs to be adapted depending on individual shoulder and arm flexibility, so always adapt for your own comfort.

1. Place your cupped hands along the back of your skull.

2. Rest the pinky ridge of your upper hand where your skull begins to curve.

3. Rest the thumb ridge of your lower hand along the occiput at the bottom of your skull.

4. Try to keep your shoulders down and relaxed. If the position is uncomfortable in a seated position, lie back with your arms and shoulders supported.

Sides of Neck

This hand position channels Reiki to your throat chakra, as well as your neck and shoulders. Some people may find this hand position needs to be adapted depending on neck length, so always adapt for your own comfort.

1. Place your cupped hands lightly on either side of your neck.

2. Rest the edges of your pinkies along the underside of your jawbone.

3. Rest the edges of your thumbs lightly on your collarbones.

4. Rest your fingertips along the sides of your neck, starting just below your earlobes.

5. Avoid pressing too hard here, as your hands will be along your carotid artery, and too much pressure can cut off or impede blood supply.

Throat and Heart

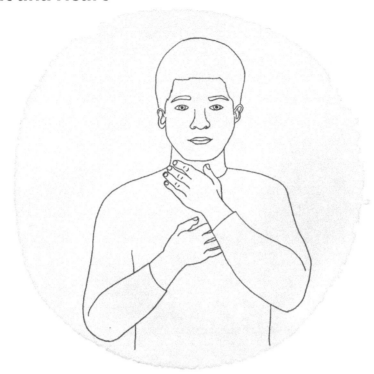

This hand position channels Reiki to your throat and heart chakras, as well as to your lungs, heart, shoulders, chest, upper thoracic vertebrae, thyroid, parathyroid, thymus gland, upper rib cage, arms, and collarbones. In this position, spread the thumb away from your upper hand while keeping your hands in the lightly cupped position. Adjust to the most comfortable position for you.

1. The base of your upper hand's palm rests lightly over your sternum at the center of your chest.

2. Separate your thumb from your fingers, resting your thumb lightly on one side of your collarbone and your fingertips lightly on the other side.

3. Cup the lower hand with the thumb tucked in, as guided previously.

4. Rest the heels of your palms lightly just off to the side of your sternum at approximately the level of the xiphoid process, with your fingertips resting upward at an angle along the side of your chest.

Ribs

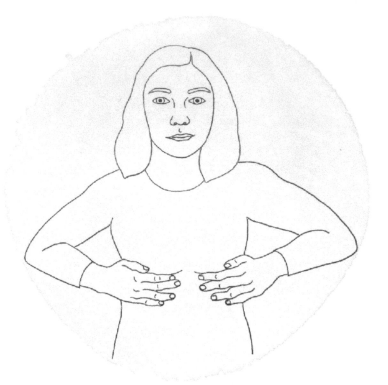

This hand position channels Reiki to your solar plexus chakra, as well as to your lower thoracic vertebrae, adrenal glands, upper abdominal organs, sternum and xiphoid process, and the lower part of your rib cage.

1. Lightly rest your fingertips of each hand along the bottom part of your sternum, with your middle fingers touching.

2. Extend your cupped hands parallel to the floor, with the heels of your palms lightly resting along your rib cage on each side.

3. Rest the edges of your pinkies along the bottom of your rib cage parallel to the floor.

Abdomen

This hand position channels Reiki to your sacral chakra, as well as to your lower abdominal organs, sexual/reproductive organs, and upper intestines.

1. Lightly place the tips of your middle fingers right on your belly button.

2. Extend your cupped hands out to either side, with the sides of your hands parallel to the floor.

Groin

This hand position channels Reiki to your sacral chakra, as well as to your hips, lower intestines, rectum, groin, and upper thighs.

1. Place your hands lightly in your lap, with your thumbs resting along the crease between your torso and your thighs.

2. Rest your hands comfortably along your thighs with your middle finger-tips touching, if possible.

Shoulders and Upper Back

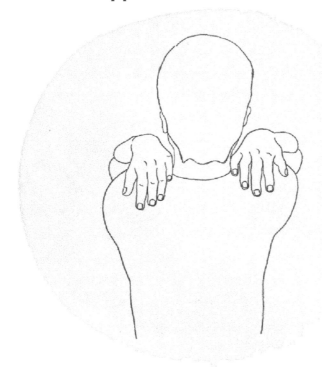

This hand position channels Reiki to your shoulders, scapulae, and upper thoracic vertebrae. Some people may find this hand position uncomfortable due to differences in flexibility, so always adapt for your own comfort. You can cross your arms in the front of your body, keep them uncrossed, do one side at a time, or lie on your back, if that makes you more comfortable.

1. Place one hand gently on each shoulder on either side of your neck.

2. Lightly rest the heels of your palms just above your collarbones on either side of your neck.

3. Wrap your fingertips over your shoulders, extending down your back perpendicular to the floor.

Middle Back

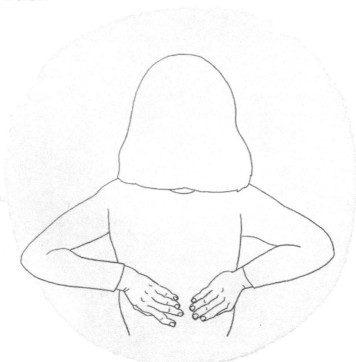

This hand position channels Reiki to your solar plexus chakra, as well as to your lower rib cage, thoracic vertebrae, and upper abdominal organs and glands including the gallbladder, liver, and adrenal glands. Some people may find this hand position uncomfortable, so always adapt for your own comfort. You might adjust to one hand at a time or do this hand position while lying on your back if it's uncomfortable to use both hands at the same time sitting in an upright position.

1. Place your middle fingertips together at your spine in the mid-thoracic region.

2. Extend your hands outward at the most comfortable angle, with the base of your palms resting lightly along the bottom part of your rib cage.

Lower Back

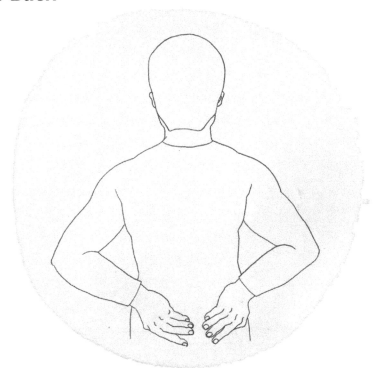

This hand position channels Reiki to your lower back, lower abdominal organs, lumbar vertebrae and tailbone, sciatic region, pelvis, and pelvic organs. Some people may find this hand position uncomfortable, so always adapt for your own comfort. You might adjust to one hand at a time or do this hand position while lying on your back if it's uncomfortable to use both hands at the same time sitting in an upright position.

1. Place your middle fingertips together comfortably along your lumbar vertebrae.

2. Rest the edges of your thumbs along the tops of your buttocks.

Knees

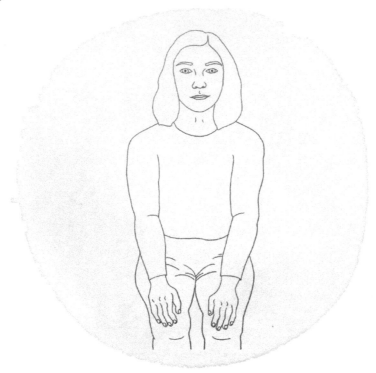

This hand position channels Reiki to your knees and upper and lower legs (thighs and calves). If possible, sit comfortably upright in this position, with your feet flat on the floor.

1. Place the base of your palms lightly on your lower thighs just above your knee joint.

2. Bend your fingers down so your fingertips rest lightly along the lower part of your kneecap (patella), just above your shins.

Feet

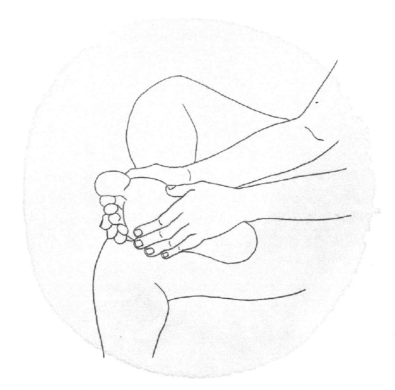

This hand position channels Reiki to your feet. Although this is listed as a single hand position, you'll actually perform it twice, once on each foot. Adjust your posture in any way that makes this a comfortable position for you to perform.

1. Cup the bottom of your foot with one hand.

2. Cup the top of your foot with the other hand.

Hand Positions for Healing Others

These hand positions for healing others work best when your healing partner is lying on an adjustable massage table at a height that is comfortable for you. Adjust the height of the table so you can sit or stand comfortably without having to lean or rest your forearms and so you can hold your hands in the positions for three to five minutes.

Using the hand positions for healing others allows you to channel Reiki to every aspect of your healing partner's body in a quick and efficient manner. Hold each position for three to five minutes. If you feel intuitively guided during a session to move your hands elsewhere, please listen to that guidance. If you're in the midst of an intuitive session and you feel your guidance stop, return to the hand positions.

To use the hand positions for healing others:

◆ Have your healing partner lie comfortably on the healing table, with their arms and legs uncrossed. Generally, they will start on their back and roll onto their stomach as the session progresses.

◆ Ask for permission to touch. If no permission is given, hover your hands a few inches above your healing partner's body.

◆ Use an extremely light touch. Avoid resting your weight or your forearms along your healing partner's body.

◆ Keep your hands cupped and thumbs tucked for all hand positions unless otherwise indicated.

Eyes

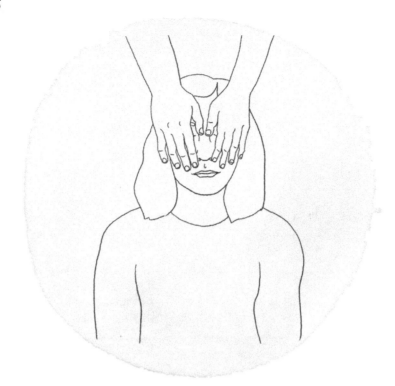

This hand position channels Reiki to your healing partner's crown and third eye chakras, as well as to their eyes, sinuses, brain, head, and pineal gland.

1. With your healing partner lying comfortably on their back, stand or sit at their head.

2. Place the base of your palms along their forehead just above their eyebrows.

3. Lightly rest your fingertips along their cheekbones.

Ears

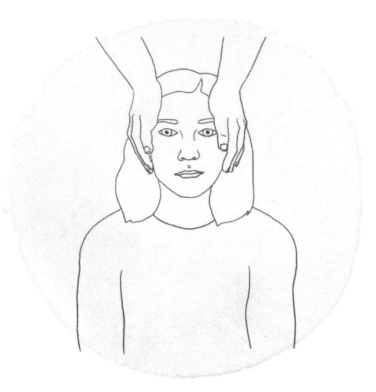

This hand position channels Reiki to your healing partner's crown and third eye chakras, as well as to their ears, brain, jaw, cheeks, mouth and teeth, and pineal gland.

1. With your healing partner lying comfortably on their back, stand or sit at their head.

2. Lightly hook your pinkies behind their ears.

3. Rest the heels of your palms gently along their temples.

4. Rest your fingertips gently along the sides of their jawbone.

Back of Head

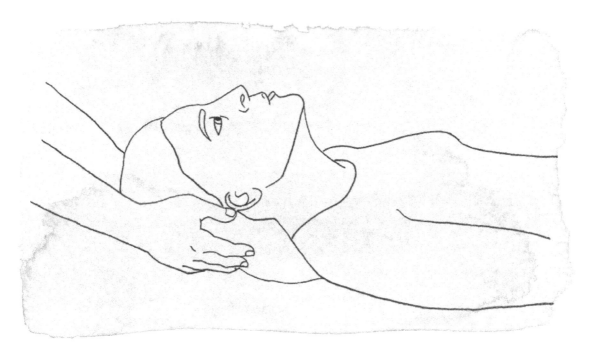

This hand position channels Reiki to your healing partner's crown and third eye chakras, as well as to their skull, brain, pineal gland, and upper vertebrae of their neck. If you do not have permission to touch, you will need to skip this hand position or have your healing partner lie on their stomach so you can hover your hands. The body holds a lot of tension here, so this is an especially beneficial hand position for people experiencing tension headaches. In this position, many people will try to hold their head up to take the weight from your hands. If you notice them holding tension in their neck in this position, wiggle your fingers gently and ask them to allow you to hold their head.

1. With your healing partner lying down, stand or sit at their head.

2. Place the sides of your pinkies together and cradle your their head in your hands.

3. Make sure you take the full weight of their head.

4. Gently rest your fingertips along their occipital ridge and the heels of your hands along the top of their skull as it starts to curve.

Throat

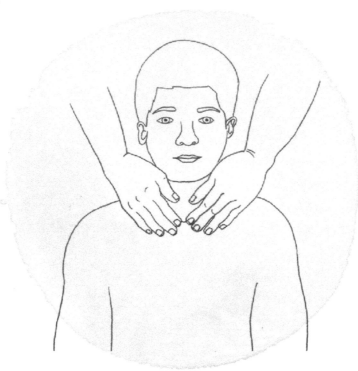

This hand position channels Reiki to your healing partner's throat chakra, as well as to their thyroid and parathyroid, neck vertebrae, collarbones, shoulders, arms, and upper chest region. This hand position may be triggering for some healing partners with a history of certain types of trauma, so be careful with it. When I ask for permission to touch, I always tell my healing partner that this is one of the hand positions I may use and ask if they would be comfortable with it. If they are not, hover your hands instead of touching them directly.

1. With your healing partner lying comfortably on their back, stand or sit at their head.

2. Rest the thumb side of your hands just below their jawbone.

3. Rest the sides of your pinkies along their collarbones.

4. Use a very light touch in this region.

Heart

This hand position channels Reiki to your healing partner's heart chakra, as well as to their heart, lungs, sternum, upper rib cage, and upper thoracic region. This hand position may be triggering for some healing partners, so be careful with it. When I ask for permission to touch, I always tell my healing partner that this is one of the hand positions I may use and ask if they would be comfortable with it. If they are not, hover your hands instead of touching them directly.

1. With your healing partner lying comfortably on their back, stand or sit at their head.

2. Place the heel of one palm lightly in the center of your healing partner's chest along the sternum, with your fingers extending at an angle upward so your fingertips rest lightly above their breast.

3. Place the heel of your other palm along their collarbone, with your fingers extending downward overlapping your other hand.

Solar Plexus

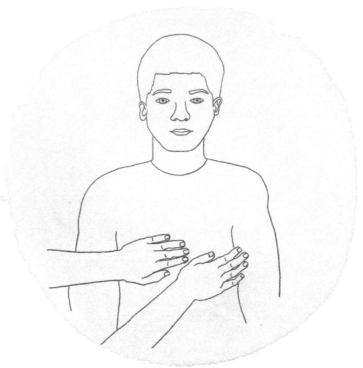

This hand position channels Reiki to your healing partner's solar plexus chakra, as well as to their adrenal glands, upper abdominal organs, rib cage, sternum, xiphoid process, and thoracic region.

1. With your healing partner lying comfortably on their back, stand or sit to one side of them.

2. Place the middle fingertip of one hand on your healing partner's xiphoid process and extend your hand perpendicular to their sternum, with the heel of your palm resting lightly along their rib cage.

3. Place the heel of your other hand up against the fingertips of your first hand and extend your hand out parallel so your fingers are resting lightly on their rib cage.

4. You may need to experiment with which hand is the most comfortable in which position.

Navel

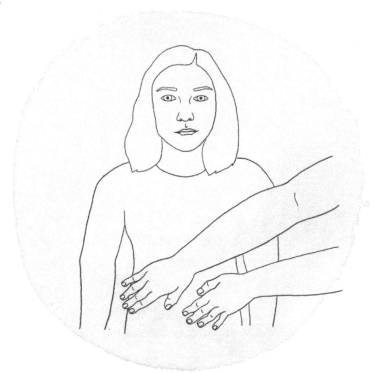

This hand position channels Reiki to your healing partner's sacral chakra, as well as to their abdominal organs, lower thoracic region, bottom of the rib cage, upper intestines, and sexual organs.

1. With your healing partner lying comfortably on their back, stand or sit to the side of them.

2. Place the middle fingertip of one hand on your healing partner's belly button.

3. Extend your hand perpendicular to their rib cage, with the heel of your hand resting lightly along your healing partner's side.

4. Place the heel of your other palm along the tip of your middle finger from the other hand.

5. Extend your fingers forward so they rest on your healing partner's other side.

6. You may need to experiment with which hand is most comfortable in which position.

Hara

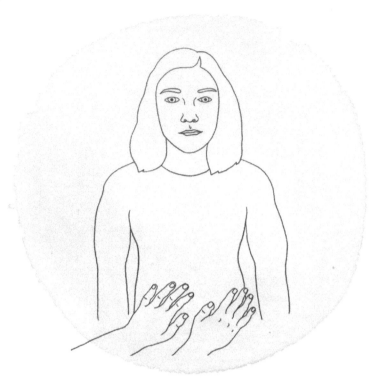

This hand position channels Reiki to your healing partner's hara, as well as to their mid-abdominal organs, upper intestines, and sexual organs. Your hara is the center point of energetic balance in your body, and it sits just below your navel.

1. With your healing partner lying comfortably on their back, stand or sit to the side of them.

2. Rest the thumb side of one hand just below their belly button, with your palm extending out to one side.

3. Rest the heel of your other hand with the thumb side lightly touching the index finger of the first hand. Extend your fingertips out to your healing partner's side.

Groin

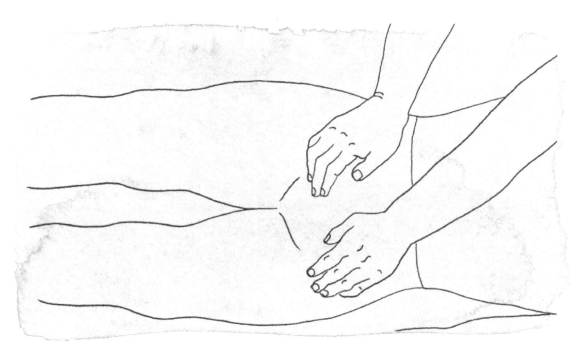

This hand position channels Reiki to your healing partner's root chakra, as well as to their groin region, lower intestines, sex organs, pelvis, pelvic organs, and upper thighs. This hand position may be triggering for some healing partners, so be careful with it. When I ask for permission to touch, I always tell my healing partner that this is one of the hand positions I may use and ask if they would be comfortable with it. If they are not, hover your hands instead of touching them directly.

1. With your healing partner lying comfortably on their back, stand or sit to the side of them.

2. Place each hand in the crease where the torso meets the hips in the position that is most comfortable for you and your healing partner.

3. Your hands should extend outward, perpendicular to their outer thighs.

Knees

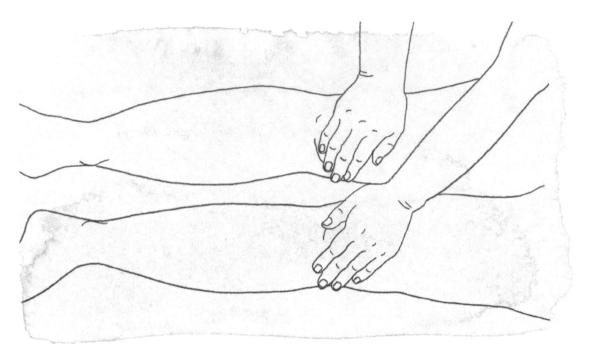

This hand position channels Reiki to your healing partner's knees and legs.

1. With your healing partner lying comfortably on their back, stand or sit to the side of them, even with their knees.

2. Place one hand over each of their knees, resting your fingertips and palms on either side of the kneecap (patella).

Ankles

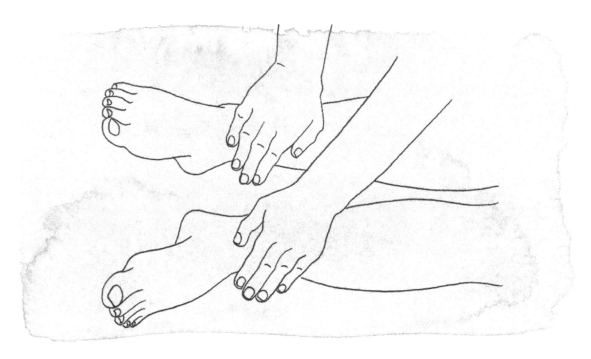

This hand position channels Reiki to your healing partner's ankles, shins, calves, and Achilles tendons.

1. With your healing partner lying comfortably on their back, stand or sit to the side of them, even with their ankles.

2. Place your hands gently over the fronts of their ankles, with your palm resting on one side and your fingertips on the other.

Feet

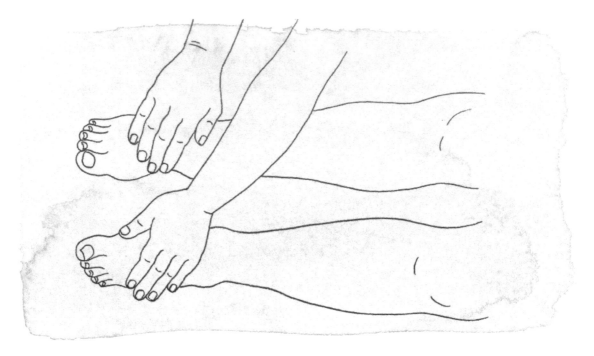

This hand position channels Reiki energy to your healing partner's feet.

1. With your healing partner lying comfortably on their back, stand or sit to the side of them, even with their feet.

2. Place the palms of your hands over the top of each of their feet, with the heels of each hand on one side of their feet and the fingertips cupped and touching the other side of their feet.

Shoulders and Upper Back

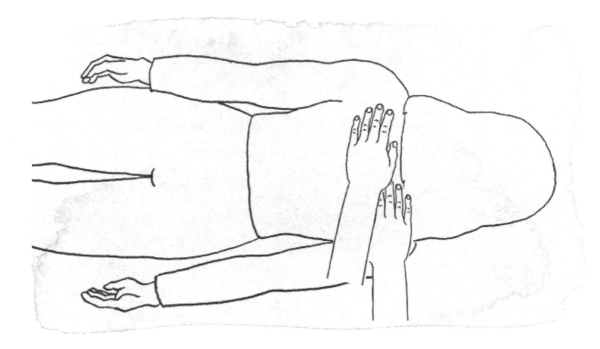

This hand position channels Reiki to your healing partner's neck, upper back, spine, lungs, heart, upper rib cage, shoulders, and scapulae. To perform the remaining hand positions, ask your healing partner to roll onto their stomach, with their legs and ankles uncrossed. Their arms can be at their sides or folded above their head.

1. With your healing partner lying comfortably on their stomach, stand or sit to the side of them, even with their shoulders.

2. Place the middle fingertip of one hand along their upper thoracic vertebrae at shoulder height, with the heel of your hand extending perpendicular to their spine and resting along their shoulders.

3. Place the palm of your other hand so it is touching the fingertip of your first hand and extends perpendicular to their spine, with your fingertips lightly resting on the back of their shoulder.

Middle Back

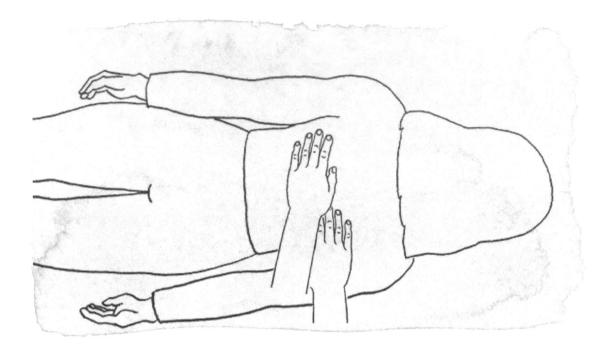

This hand position channels Reiki to your healing partner's middle back region, thoracic spine, heart, lungs, and mid portion of the rib cage.

1. With your healing partner lying comfortably on their stomach, stand or sit to the side of them, even with their mid-thoracic region.

2. Place the middle fingertip of one hand along a thoracic vertebra (near where the bra strap lies on a woman).

3. Extend your hand perpendicular to their spine, with the heel of that hand resting lightly on their rib cage.

4. Place the heel of your other hand against the middle fingertip and extend your fingers perpendicular to their spine to rest your fingertips of that hand along their rib cage.

Lower Back

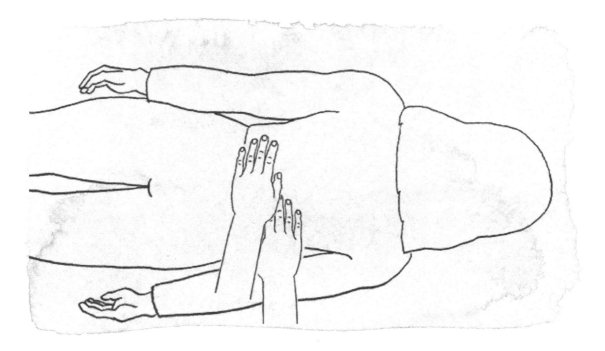

This hand position channels Reiki to your healing partner's lumbar region, tailbone, sexual organs, hips, and pelvis.

1. With your healing partner lying comfortably on their stomach, stand or sit to the side of them, even with their pelvis.

2. Place the middle fingertip of one hand along a lumber vertebra so that the bottom of your hand skims along their buttock, running perpendicular to their spine, with the heel of your hand touching their side.

3. Place the heel of your other hand at the tip of the middle finger of your first hand. Extend the hand perpendicular to their spine so your fingertips touch their other side.

Tops of Legs

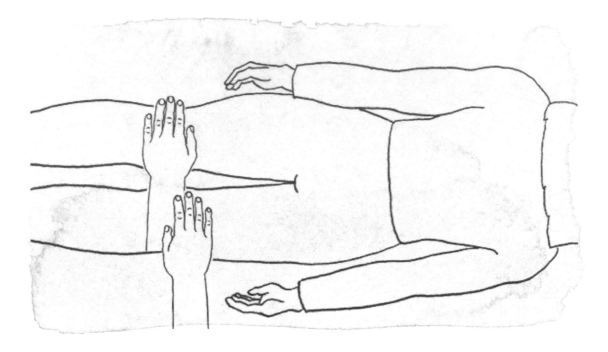

This hand position channels Reiki to your healing partner's root chakra, tailbone, rectum, and hamstrings.

1. With your healing partner lying comfortably on their stomach, stand or sit to the side of them, even with their buttocks.

2. Place one hand along the crease of where their buttocks meets their hamstrings, extending perpendicular to their spine, with your fingertips lightly touching their inner thigh and the base of your palm lightly touching their other thigh.

3. For the other hand, place it in a similar position along their other thigh.

Clearing the Aura

Sweep your healing partner's aura at the beginning and end of every Reiki healing session. Sweeping the aura helps remove any energetic disturbances in your healing partner's energetic field and grounds and sets the changes from a Reiki session in the body. To sweep the aura:

1. Have your healing partner sit on the edge of the healing table or stand next to the table.

2. Stand facing your healing partner.

3. Beginning at the top of the head 2 to 3 inches above their crown chakra, sweep one or both hands along the contours of their body, down toward the floor, maintaining a few inches of distance between your hands and your healing partner.

4. At the end of each sweep, touch the floor with your hands to ground the energy.

5. Sweep 4 or 5 times, always starting at the crown of their head and moving downward, moving around all planes of your healing partner's body.

Bridge Position

The bridge hand position allows you to move Reiki from one area to another with the placement of your hands. For example, if someone gets lots of creative ideas (born in the sacral chakra) but has trouble expressing them (throat chakra), then you may wish to create a Reiki bridge to connect the sacral chakra to the throat chakra. To do this, you place one hand over the throat chakra and the other hand over the sacral chakra and visualize the Reiki energy flowing between the two. You can use this position—with one hand in one position and the other in another—to connect energy anywhere you feel it isn't flowing properly.

Hand Positions for Quick Healing

Sometimes you or your healing partner lack the time (or the table) to do a full Reiki session. In such cases, you can always complete a quick healing session, in which you have your healing partner sit in a chair with their bare feet flat on the floor and you pursue hand positions for one to five minutes that cover each chakra as well as the knees and feet. This allows Reiki to go where it's needed without taking as much time as a traditional session.

Hands on Shoulders

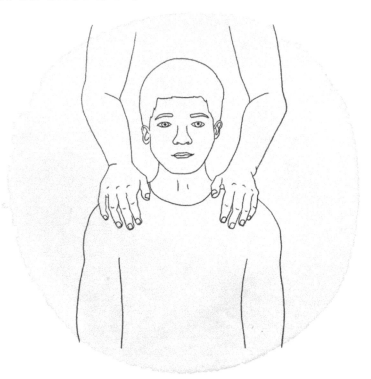

This hand position allows you and your healing partner to get used to each other's energy and start the Reiki process for a quick session.

1. Stand up straight behind your healing partner.

2. Place one hand gently on each of your healing partner's shoulders with the heels of your palms resting on the backs of their shoulder blades and your fingertips resting on their collarbones.

Crown Chakra

This hand position channels Reiki to the crown chakra and all areas of the body it affects, including the brain, head, skin, and skeletal system.

1. Stand behind your healing partner.

2. Hold your hands cupped over the crown of your healing partner's head, hovering them 2 to 4 inches above.

Third Eye Chakra

This hand position channels Reiki to the third eye chakra and all areas of the body it affects, including the brain, sinuses, and eyes.

1. Stand to the side of your healing partner.

2. Place one hand across their forehead running parallel to their brow.

3. Place your other hand across the back of their head at the same height in a similar position.

Throat Chakra

This hand position channels Reiki to the throat chakra and all areas of the body it affects, including the thyroid, neck, jaw, ears, and parathyroid. This hand position may be triggering for some healing partners, so be careful with it. When I ask for permission to touch, I always tell my healing partner that this is one of the hand positions I may use and ask if they would be comfortable with it. If they are not, hover your hands instead of touching them directly.

1. Stand to the side of your healing partner.

2. Place one hand lightly and gently over their throat chakra, running parallel to their chin.

3. Place your other hand along the back of their neck in a similar position.

Heart Chakra

This hand position channels Reiki to the heart chakra and all areas of the body it affects, including the heart, lungs, and ribs.

1. Stand or kneel (depending on which is most comfortable for you) to one side of your healing partner.

2. Place one hand in the center of their chest, with the pinkie edge of your hand running just along the tops of their breasts parallel to the floor.

3. Place your other hand along the back of their body in a similar position.

Solar Plexus Chakra

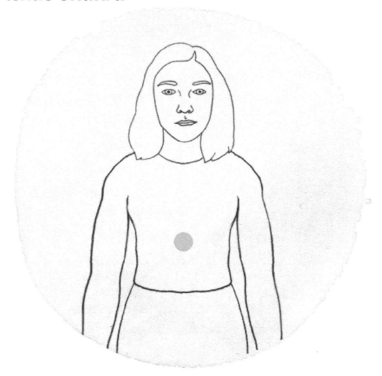

This hand position channels Reiki to the solar plexus chakra and all areas of the body it affects, including the rib cage, adrenal glands, middle back, and upper abdominal organs.

1. Sit, stand, or kneel to one side of your healing partner.

2. Place one hand over their solar plexus chakra, with your palm directly over their solar plexus. Extend your fingers parallel to the floor so they fall just underneath their breast.

3. Place your other hand along their back in a similar position.

Sacral Chakra

This hand position channels Reiki to the sacral chakra and all areas of the body it affects, including the abdominal organs, sexual organs, and lumbar spine.

1. Sit or kneel to one side of your healing partner.

2. Place one hand along the front of their body with the thumb side of your hand running just underneath their belly button and your hand running parallel to the floor.

3. Place your other hand along the back of their body in a similar position.

Root Chakra

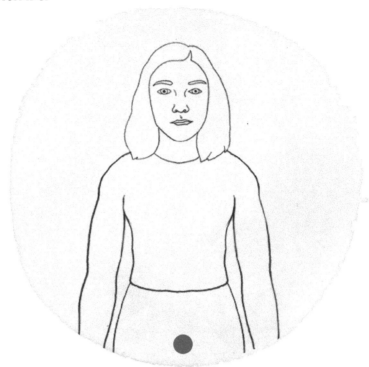

This hand position channels Reiki to the root chakra and all areas of the body it affects, including the pelvis, colon, sciatic region, tailbone, and hips.

1. Sit in front of your healing partner on the floor, facing them.

2. Place each hand along the tops of their thighs in the crease where the thigh meets the torso, with the heel of your hands on their outer thighs and your fingertips on their inner thighs.

Knees

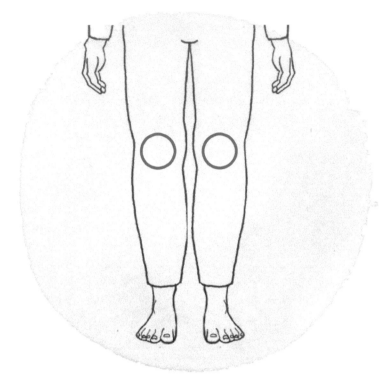

This hand position channels Reiki to the knees and legs.

1. Sit in front of your healing partner on the floor, facing them.

2. Place each hand along the tops of their knees, with your fingertips resting on the inside of their knees and the palms of your hands resting on the outside.

Feet

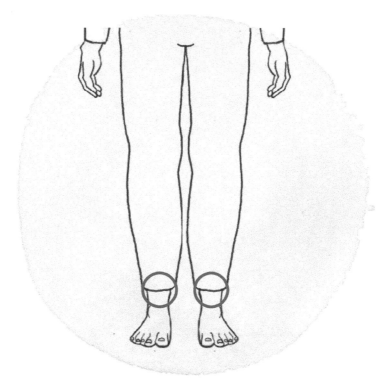

This hand position channels Reiki to the feet and ankles.

1. Sit on the floor in front of your healing partner, facing them.

2. Place each hand along the tops of one of your healing partner's feet, with the heels of your hands resting on the outside of their arches and your fingertips resting on the inside of their arches.

CHAPTER FOUR

Reiki Sequences for Physical Health

In this chapter, you'll find common Reiki sequences to help with common physical ailments. These sequences are not a substitute for proper medical care, but they can serve as an adjunct to it and help spur the healing process. And though the ailments treated here are physical, the Reiki sequences seek to support the energetic issues that may lead to such illnesses as well as help manage the symptoms associated with dis-ease. It's important to remember that as a Reiki practitioner, you should never diagnose a healing partner, nor should you counteract or oppose any doctor's recommendations. Your role is to support your healing partner as they work with the energetic conditions surrounding their dis-ease.

For all sequences, hold each hand position for three to five minutes, or until you notice signs of release. Your healing partner should be lying on their back unless otherwise indicated. End each session by sweeping their aura and having your healing partner sip from a glass of cool water for grounding.

Migraine Headaches

According to the Migraine Research Foundation, migraines are the third most prevalent medical condition in the world, affecting about 12 percent of the population, including men, women, and children of all ages. Migraines can present in many different ways—from "classic" migraine headaches with auras that precede them to less common ocular migraines. Migraines may have a cluster of triggers that can range from infrequent and mild to chronic and severe.

Affected Chakras

- Crown
- Third eye
- Throat
- Heart
- Solar plexus
- Sacral

Step-by-Step Instructions

1. Make sure the lights are low and any music is soft. For all hand positions, use an extremely light touch.

2. Stand at your healing partner's head and hold the following sequence of hand positions: Eyes – Ears – Back of Head – Throat.

3. Move to your healing partner's side and hold the following hand positions: Heart – Solar Plexus – Navel.

4. Ask your healing partner to roll onto their stomach and, standing at their side, complete the following hand positions: Shoulders and Upper Back-Middle Back.

Tip:

- If you have an essential oil diffuser, diffuse lavender essential oil, which can be helpful for headaches and creates a relaxing, peaceful atmosphere.
- An amethyst crystal placed on the third eye chakra can help with migraine energy.

Autoimmune Disease

According to the American Autoimmune Related Diseases Association, there are more than 100 different autoimmune diseases affecting different body parts, organs, and systems. Common autoimmune diseases include type 1 diabetes, asthma, rheumatoid arthritis, psoriasis, lupus, celiac disease, Graves' disease, and Hashimoto's thyroiditis.

Affected Chakras

Two primary chakras affect autoimmune disease—the crown chakra and the root chakra. Generally, there's also a third chakra involved, which is the chakra supporting the location in the body where the disease symptoms manifest (such as the solar plexus chakra/pancreas in type 1 diabetes). The following lists some of the affected chakras for common forms of autoimmune disease.

▶ Crown—lupus, psoriasis, rheumatoid arthritis, scleroderma
▶ Third eye—multiple sclerosis, ankylosing spondylitis, amyotrophic lateral sclerosis (ALS), narcolepsy
▶ Throat—Graves' disease, Hashimoto's thyroiditis
▶ Heart—rheumatic heart disease, arthritis, autoimmune myocarditis, asthma
▶ Solar plexus—type 1 diabetes, autoimmune hepatitis
▶ Sacral—endometriosis, interstitial cystitis
▶ Root—celiac disease, irritable bowel syndrome, gout

Step-by-Step Instructions

1. Stand at your healing partner's side. Hold the following hand positions: Hara – Groin.

2. Stand at your healing partner's head. Hold the following hand positions: Eyes – Ears – Back of Head – (chakra associated with symptoms of autoimmune disease).

3. Hold a series of bridge hand positions with one hand on each location:

- Hara – Crown (from Quick Healing Hand Positions—hand on crown of head)
- Hara – Third Eye (from Quick Healing Hand Positions—hand on forehead)
- Hara – chakra associated with autoimmune disease
- Crown – chakra associated with autoimmune disease (from Quick Healing Hand Positions)

Tip: Snowflake obsidian is an excellent crystal to use as you work with someone who has autoimmune disease, as it connects root and crown chakra energy, allowing for better flow of energy through all the chakras. During treatment, place a piece of snowflake obsidian under the treatment table or on the treatment table at about hara height next to your healing partner.

Anxiety

Anxiety disorders affect more than 18 percent of the American population, according to the Anxiety and Depression Association of America. Anxiety disorders can take multiple forms, such as generalized anxiety, social anxiety, phobias, and obsessive-compulsive disorders, just to name a few. Anxiety disorders can have both physical and mental causes, but the effects of the disorder often manifest physically.

Affected Chakras

- Third eye
- Solar plexus
- Root

Step-by-Step Instructions

1. Start at your healing partner's head and hold the following hand positions: Eyes – Ears – Back of Head.

2. Move to your healing partner's side and hold the following hand positions: Solar Plexus – Navel – Hara – Groin.

3. At the end of the session, have your healing partner stand with their bare feet flat on the floor to sweep their aura and ground the anxiety.

Tip: During the session, ask your healing partner to focus on this deep, calming breathing pattern:

- Inhale deeply through your nose into your abdomen for a count of 4.
- Hold the inhale for a count of 4.
- Exhale through your mouth for a slow count of 8, expelling all your air.

Your healing partner can return to this breathing pattern in their daily life when they feel their anxiety arise.

Additionally, if your healing partner is in a calm and relaxed state at the end of a Reiki session, you can teach them a simple technique from neuro-linguistic programming (NLP) called *anchoring* to recall their relaxed state when they start to feel anxious again. After grounding your healing partner as noted previously:

◆ Have them create some type of a gesture (such as touching the tips of their middle finger and thumb together in a circle like an okay sign).
◆ Have them hold the gesture for one or two minutes, or until their state of calm relaxation begins to fade. This anchors the feeling of peace and calm in the gesture.
◆ Now, whenever they feel anxiety arising, they can repeat the gesture to recall the feeling they had at the end of the Reiki session.

Arthritis

The Centers for Disease Control and Prevention notes that more than 54 million adults in the United States (about 23 percent) have some form of arthritis, with the most common form being osteoarthritis. Arthritis is caused by inflammation of the joints, and the condition can be painful and debilitating.

Affected Chakras

- ▸ Crown
- ▸ Root

Step-by-Step Instructions

Along with treating the crown and root chakras, you will also want to hold hand positions over the locations where the arthritis is most prevalent. For example, if your healing partner presents with arthritis in the shoulders, then one of your hand positions should be a nontraditional hand position where you stand at your healing partner's head with your hands over each shoulder. Use a very light touch to avoid making symptoms worse.

1. Stand at your healing partner's side and hold the following hand positions: Hara – Groin.

2. Stand at your healing partner's head and hold the following hand positions: Eyes – Ears – Back of Head.

3. Hold your hands very lightly over the area where the pain manifests, such as hands, ankles, elbows, shoulders, or knees.

Tip: Sea salt or Himalayan pink salt baths are especially beneficial for people suffering from arthritis. Encourage your healing partner to take 10-minute warm baths with a quarter cup of Himalayan pink salt or sea salt dissolved in the water 3 to 5 times per week, as well as during periods of pain and immediately following a Reiki session.

Hypertension

According to the World Health Organization, about 1.13 billion people worldwide experience hypertension, also known as high blood pressure. Hypertension is often a symptomless physical issue, but the results of long-term untreated hypertension can be catastrophic, leading to heart attack, heart failure, and other life-threatening physical health problems.

Affected Chakras

▸ Crown
▸ Heart
▸ Solar plexus

Step-by-Step Instructions

1. Stand at your healing partner's head and hold the following hand positions: Eyes – Ears – Back of Head.

2. Move to your healing partner's side and hold the following hand positions: Heart – Solar Plexus.

3. Next, have your healing partner roll onto their stomach and complete the following hand positions: Shoulders and Upper Back – Middle Back – Lower Back.

Tip: Always encourage your healing partner to follow their doctor's instructions for treatment of hypertension. High blood pressure is a function of overactive heart energy, so working with opaque crystals that support heart energy can help absorb some of the excess energy. Choose an opaque green crystal, such as jade or ruby in fuchsite. Place the crystal directly over the heart chakra as you channel Reiki energy through the stone into heart chakra.

Metabolic Syndrome

Metabolic syndrome is a cluster of symptoms and conditions that occur together, according to the Mayo Clinic. These conditions can increase your risk of health issues such as type 2 diabetes, heart disease, and stroke. Conditions that make up metabolic syndrome include high blood pressure, excess body fat around the middle, high blood sugar, and high cholesterol or triglycerides.

Affected Chakras

▸ Crown
▸ Heart
▸ Solar plexus

Step-by-Step Instructions

1. Stand at your healing partner's head and hold the following hand positions: Eyes – Ears – Back of Head.

2. Move to your healing partner's side and hold the following hand positions: Heart – Solar Plexus.

3. If your healing partner has issues associated with type 2 diabetes, such as neuropathy, also use the following hand positions: Groin – Knees – Ankles – Feet.

4. Next, have your healing partner roll onto their stomach and complete the following hand positions: Middle Back – Lower Back.

5. At the end of the session, have your healing partner stand with their bare feet flat on the floor.

6. Sweep your healing partner's aura, visualizing the unhealthy energy you have cleared as black shadows flowing down through the body as your hands sweep, draining through the soles of the feet into the Earth, where it is neutralized.

Tip: Grapefruit and peppermint essential oils can help with symptoms associated with metabolic disorder. Diffuse one or both of these oils during the session.

Fibromyalgia

Fibromyalgia is a painful cluster of symptoms that is still poorly understood. According to the American Chronic Pain Association, fibromyalgia affects roughly 2 to 4 percent of the population, with an overwhelming majority of people with fibromyalgia being women (about 90 percent). Research into this debilitating illness is ongoing, but some research suggests the causes may be neurological.

Affected Chakras

▶ All

Step-by-Step Instructions

Hands-on healing, if tolerated, is especially helpful for fibromyalgia because the warmth from the hands is soothing to pain. However, it is important you use a very light touch to avoid aggravating pain points. In spots where touch is not tolerated, hover your hands 2 to 3 inches above the body.

1. Stand at your healing partner's head and hold the following hand positions: Eyes – Ears.

2. Move to your healing partner's side and hold the following hand positions: Heart – Solar Plexus – Navel – Groin – Knees – Ankles – Feet.

3. Next, have your healing partner roll onto their stomach and complete the following hand positions: Shoulders and Upper Back – Middle Back – Lower Back – Tops of Legs.

4. While your healing partner is on their stomach, use a bridge position with one hand at the base of the spine held over the coccyx, and one hand gently resting at the top of the head.

Tip: During your session, ask your healing partner to visualize any pain points as black shadows that drain out of their body through the table and into the Earth, where the pain is neutralized.

Menstrual Issues

Menstrual issues are common for women and can present with a range of symptoms. Some common menstrual issues women experience include painful periods, extremely heavy periods, absent periods, issues associated with menopause, irregular menstruation, and fibroids. All have similar energetic causes, so regardless of the way they present, you can manage the energetics of the issues in the same manner.

Affected Chakras

Menstrual issues are primarily associated with the sacral chakra, which controls the sexual organs.

- Third eye
- Throat
- Heart
- Sacral
- Root

Step-by-Step Instructions

In this sequence, instead of working from the top down, as you would in other health issues, you work from the bottom up. This raises the vibration through the chakras.

1. Stand at your healing partner's side and hold the following hand positions: Groin – Hara – Navel – Heart.

2. Move to your healing partner's head and hold the following hand positions: Throat – Back of Head – Ears – Eyes.

3. If your healing partner experiences back pain as part of their menstrual issues, have them roll onto their stomach and hold the following hand positions: Top of Legs – Lower Back – Middle Back.

Tip: Place a piece of carnelian on your healing partner's sacral chakra throughout the treatment while they lie on their back. You can also diffuse orange essential oil to help support sacral chakra energy throughout the session.

Indigestion/Gastroesophageal Reflux Disease

About one out of four people are affected with indigestion, according to the National Institutes of Health's National Institute of Diabetes and Digestive and Kidney Diseases. Indigestion can be occasional and mild, or it can be chronic and severe. Many severe cases are caused by gastroesophageal reflux disease (GERD), which arises from a malfunction of the lower esophageal sphincter (LES) that allows gastric acid into the chest and throat.

Affected Chakras

- Throat
- Heart
- Solar plexus
- Sacral

Step-by-Step Instructions

Place a pillow under your healing partner's head and shoulders to help manage the symptoms associated with GERD during the treatment.

1. Stand at your healing partner's head and hold the following hand position: Throat.

2. Move to your healing partner's side and hold the following hand positions: Heart – Solar Plexus – Navel – Hara.

Tip: GERD and acid reflux are associated with too much of the chi element of fire. Certain food and beverages—including spicy foods (such as chiles), coffee, and alcoholic beverages—are associated with increasing the fire element. Your healing partner may want to avoid them. Instead, suggest they enjoy cooling foods such as yogurt and berries and drinking room temperature to cool (but not cold) water.

Thyroid Disease

Although some thyroid diseases—such as Hashimoto's thyroiditis and Graves' disease—are autoimmune, others are not. For autoimmune thyroid disease, you can follow the autoimmune protocols on page 94, paying special attention to the throat chakra. This sequence can support both autoimmune and nonautoimmune thyroid disease.

Affected Chakras

▶ Crown
▶ Third eye
▶ Throat
▶ Solar plexus
▶ Sacral

Step-by-Step Instructions

Nonautoimmune thyroid disease is a malfunction of your body's endocrine system, which produces hormones throughout your body. Imbalances in one hormone (such as thyroid hormones) can have a cascading effect, leading to imbalances in other hormones as well.

1. Stand at your healing partner's head and hold the following hand positions: Eyes – Ears – Back of Head – Throat.

2. Move to your healing partner's side and hold the following hand positions: Solar Plexus – Navel – Hara.

3. Next, ask your healing partner to roll onto their stomach and work in the following order: Shoulders and Upper Back – Middle Back.

4. While your healing partner is on their stomach, use a bridge position with one hand at the Lower Back position, and one hand on the Shoulders and Upper Back position. Visualize the energy rising from your Lower Back hand to your Shoulders and Upper Back hand, clearing any blockages in energy along its path as it rises.

Tip: Teach your healing partner the Bija mantra (a single-syllable mantra that activates the energy for each chakra) for the throat chakra, which has Ham (pronounced "hahmmmmmmmm"). If your healing partner feels comfortable doing so, have them chant Ham as you channel Reiki to their throat chakra. If they aren't comfortable doing so, suggest that they spend five minutes each day with their hands resting lightly on their throat chakra chanting this mantra.

PART TWO

Second Degree Reiki

In this part, you will learn everything you need to know as a Second Degree Reiki practitioner. Second Degree Reiki allows you to channel a more powerful form of Reiki and provides you with attunements, skills, and knowledge that allows you to send Reiki across time and space, such as to someone across the room or on the other side of the world, as well as to the past and the future.

CHAPTER FIVE

Second Degree Reiki Training

Second Degree Reiki (Okuden) steps up your healing ability so you can open a professional Reiki practice, if that's your goal. First Degree Reiki is "friends and family Reiki" and deals with hands-on, in-person Reiki practice. Learning the Second Degree Reiki fundamentals and being attuned to the Second Degree energy and symbols opens up your practice, allowing you to use a more powerful form of Reiki energy that you can channel not only in-person and hands-on but also across time and space. This distance healing ability opens numerous possibilities for Reiki healing and makes you a more well-rounded energy healer. In this chapter, you'll learn the fundamentals of Second Degree Reiki.

What to Expect in Second Degree Reiki Training

At the end of Second Degree Reiki training, you'll be attuned to the Second Degree Reiki energy, a more powerful form of Reiki energy than First Degree. You'll also learn how to draw and use the traditional Usui Ryoho Reiki symbols for physical, mental, emotional, spiritual, and distance healing, bringing more power and focus to your sessions. Once you are attuned to the Second Degree Reiki energy and symbols, you are attuned to them for life.

Deeper Healing Opportunities

With a more powerful form of Reiki energy flowing, you have the opportunity to provide a higher vibration of energy healing. Second Degree energy is more focused and often works more quickly than First Degree energy.

Distance Healing

Freed from the constraints of time and space, the opportunities for sharing healing energy are endless. This opens a world of possibilities that aren't available to First Degree Reiki practitioners. Working with Second Degree Energy and the Reiki distance healing symbol (page 124) allows you to channel Reiki energy across time and space; fill entire spaces with Reiki energy; channel healing energy to situations such as natural disasters or pandemics; provide Reiki to people, animals, plants, or objects that can't be in your physical space; and even channel Reiki energy to entire groups of people or the planet as a whole. Additionally, you can send Reiki back into the past or forward into the future to help heal issues that may contribute to disease.

Spiritual Development

Attunement to and channeling of Second Degree Reiki energy also provides opportunities for spiritual growth.

- You may experience greater intuition because Second Degree Reiki focuses on intuitive healing.
- Many Reiki practitioners also begin working with their Reiki guides during this degree.
- Second Degree practitioners also notice that their own personal energy vibrates at a higher frequency that provides a deeper connection to universal (Source) energy.
- Second Degree Reiki practices encourage deeper spiritual awareness through meditation, seeking guidance from higher sources, and developing a set of ethics about energy healing focused on serving the highest good.

Healing Past Lives

With the ability to channel Reiki across time and space, Second Degree Reiki practitioners can also channel universal Reiki energy in ways that allow both the practitioner and their healing partners to deal with karmic issues arising from past lives, lives between lives, and their actions in this life. Karmic issues frequently appear in our daily lives in forms of energetic imbalance and dis-ease that offer each of us the opportunity to discover those issues, work through them, and create a new, balanced state of being that serves our greatest good.

Second Degree Attunements

You can receive your Second Degree attunement in-person or at a distance. You must already be attuned to First Degree Reiki, and a Reiki Master-Teacher must complete the attunement. During the attunement, you will be attuned to Second Degree Reiki energy and to three Second Degree Reiki symbols. Attunement to this energy and these symbols allows you to deepen your practice.

After a Second Degree attunement, the Reiki energy you channel will have a greater intensity. Because of this increase, just as you experienced during your First Degree attunement, you will have a 21-day period of adjustment in which you may experience some mild symptoms of body, mind, and spirit as you adapt to having a higher frequency energy flowing through you. During these 21 days, continue to channel Reiki to yourself daily by using a full hands-on healing session you learned in chapter 3, or by channeling Reiki to yourself for at least five minutes every day.

As with your First Degree attunement, you may also notice psychic changes such as deeper levels of intuition, liberating shifts in your emotional framework, more intense dreams, and positive changes in your physical, emotional, mental, and spiritual health. Most of my students report to me that with each successive attunement, they feel more "tuned-in" to intuitive information, and they feel they can dial into the Reiki energy more quickly and efficiently. Many also report that they feel more connected to universal energy as well as to their healing partners.

Common Psychic Gifts

I believe everyone is intuitive, and what differentiates people called "psychics" from people who don't believe they are psychic is simply that those using their psychic abilities have learned to understand them and have developed them by working with their intuitive gifts. In other words, although I identify as a psychic because I have learned to recognize, understand, and work with those gifts, I am no different from anyone reading this book. You also have intuitive gifts that, with attention and practice, you can develop into psychic gifts. Developing these gifts is invaluable to Reiki practitioners of all degrees.

There are different ways people might experience psychic information, so the first step is understanding the various ways your intuition might manifest. Then, you can begin to work with that information in safe situations, such as during a Reiki session or with a loved one, to strengthen your psychic "muscle."

Clairaudience (Auditory Psychic Information)

Clairaudience, or psychic hearing, is a common way people receive psychic information, and it's more than just "hearing voices," although that can be part of the ability or gift.

Clairaudience can manifest in a variety of ways. Often, the first way it manifests that people can recognize is through a sense of pressure in the ears, such as how it feels when your ears might need to pop as you ascend or descend in an airplane. If you notice such a sensation, pay attention and see if you notice any of the following forms of clairaudient information:

- Hearing words or phrases in your mind or with your ears
- Hearing sounds such as whistling or experiencing a high-pitched ringing in your ears
- Awakening in the morning with a word, sound, or phrase ringing in your ears
- Noticing other sounds or ear sensations such as hearing musical tones, snippets of music, or bells ringing
- In a Reiki session, hearing a simple word—such as "heart," "lungs," or "leg"—directing you where to channel Reiki energy
- Experiencing other auditory sensations such as a muffling of sound, changes in pitch or frequency, rises and drops in volume, or hypersensitivity to background noise

Clairvoyance (Visual Psychic Information)

Clairvoyance is also known as psychic seeing. You may notice visions, either with your physical eyes or with your mind's eye.

Many people expect clairvoyance to be obvious images or like watching a film with their mind's eye, and for some people this is certainly the case. But for many, clairvoyance is more a series of quick, fleeting images that flash by and are gone as quickly as they came, much like flickering images on a film that flash by so fast you almost aren't aware of them. Some manifestations of clairvoyance include:

◆ Visual disturbances such as eye floaters or energy waves similar to heat waves
◆ Flashes of light or color seen either with the eye or in the mind's eye
◆ Persistent images in your mind's eye that return repeatedly or linger
◆ Flashes of images in the mind's eye that don't match anything you're thinking, seeing, or doing
◆ Shadows, figures, and visions seen either with the eye or in the mind's eye
◆ Symbols that flash in your mind

In a Reiki session, clairvoyance may manifest as a column of light or heat waves around a body part in need of Reiki energy, or it might be a vision of a specific body part in your mind's eye during the session such as seeing a rib cage or a foot flash through your brain.

Clairsentience (Somatic Psychic Intuition)

Clairsentience, or clear feeling, is about having feelings or sensations in your physical body and energy field that transmits information about other people around you. Some ways clairsentience may manifest include the following:

◆ Physical sensations in your body that tell you how another is feeling physically, such as aches and pains, tingling, etc.
◆ The ability to feel changes in energy when you scan your hands over someone else

These sensations may occur as pushes, pulls, tingling, hot or cold sensations, and similar changes in pressure felt in the palms of your hands.

Claircognizance (Psychic Knowing)

Claircognizance, or psychic knowing, is the intuitive gift of suddenly knowing information. Generally, with claircognizance, you simply have information "uploaded" to your brain all at once, and you know something you didn't know before. Claircognizance may manifest in the following ways:

◆ Sudden knowing of information you didn't know before
◆ Knowing your healing partner has an energy imbalance in a certain part of the body
◆ Suddenly knowing something about someone's history that affects their mental, physical, emotional, spiritual, or energetic health

Clairempathy (Empathy)

Clairempathy is the term for being empathic or feeling another's emotions as if they are your own. I find that many people drawn to energy healing are empaths, although they may not recognize that they are. Empaths feel other people's emotions and may have difficulty differentiating them from their own feelings. Some ways clairempathy may manifest include the following:

◆ Feeling an emotion that is unrelated to anything you are currently experiencing, such as being happy at a party and suddenly feeling sadness of no particular onset when someone approaches you
◆ Feeling drained after being in the presence of certain people
◆ Feeling a whirl of emotions, rapid mood swings, or other strong or shifting emotions in crowds

In a Reiki session, you might feel shifts in emotions unrelated to your Reiki work as you move your healing partner's energy and release trapped emotions.

Mediumship

All mediums are psychic, but not all psychics are mediums. A *medium* is someone who uses their various intuitive gifts (the "clairs" listed previously), to communicate with the spirit world. If you are a medium, your gifts may manifest in any of the ways noted—for example, a clairvoyant medium may actually be able to see spirits, whereas a clairaudient medium may hear them. Signs of mediumship may include the following:

- You had an imaginary friend when you were a child.
- You have vivid dreams about or visions of people who have died.
- You have distinct sensations in haunted locations that indicate the presence of ghosts.
- You believe or know you communicate with the dead in some way.

The Team of Light: Reiki Guides

All souls incarnated in human bodies have *spirit guides*, or beings existing in the realm of the absolute who provide guidance through dreams, intuition, and other signs. You may have one spirit guide or many. People attuned to Reiki have at least one additional specialist Reiki guide who is there to help them in their Reiki and energy healing practice.

The Role of Spirit Guides

Some of your spirit guides have been with you throughout lifetimes, whereas others may arrive during different periods of your life or lives in order to impart specific guidance and information. Your guides are not here to tell you what to do, but they are here to provide signs and information that serve your greatest good. You are never required to follow guidance from your spirit guides, although their guidance always exists to help set you on your life's path in a way that serves the highest good.

Spirit guides may play various roles in your life:

- Some arrive during a particular period to provide love and support during a difficult situation.
- Some are with you daily, providing guidance in the form of intuition, knowing, psychic information, and dreams.
- Some are "specialists," here to guide you in one aspect of your life, such as an energy healing practice, your career, or your form of artistic expression. Reiki guides fall into this category.
- Some are loved ones in your soul group (a group of souls you incarnate with over lifetimes for the purposes of karmic balance) who have died in this lifetime and wish to provide ongoing love and support.

- Some come for only a brief time to help create a situation that serves your highest good.
- Some are here to help you with specific initiatives or passions in your life, such as the pursuit of social justice or environmentalism.

Types of Spirit Guides

There are many different types of spirit guide. And although it is impossible to list all types, here are a few common ones.

TEACHER GUIDES

Teacher guides are with you in your life between lives (when you are in the spirit state) and help guide your overall growth as a spirit. Teacher guides can incarnate with you into lifetimes to help provide learning and support, or they may guide you from another dimension while you are incarnated via feelings, dreams, etc. You may recognize teacher guides in the following ways:

- A friend or family member who plays a mentorship or significant role in your life
- Someone who comes into your life for a brief period who serves as a catalyst to change everything
- A helpful mentor or teacher that appears in your dreams
- A voice of inner guidance

ANGELS

Angels are energetic entities that have never been incarnated as human beings. They are pure energetic spirits who have stepped outside of karmic cycles to provide love and support that serves the greatest good for the universe as a whole. Angels may manifest in the following ways:

- As a being of light that arrives to provide a helping hand during a period of crisis or difficult time
- As a voice of guidance during particularly difficult times
- As a being of light appearing in dreams providing insight that leads to change or growth

REIKI GUIDES

Your *Reiki guides* are spirits that exist in another dimension to help you with your energy healing practices. Many believe that past Reiki Masters are Reiki guides that help all practitioners, but each individual practitioner has their own Reiki guide or guides, too. Call on your Reiki guides for assistance during Reiki sessions. Support from Reiki guides may manifest in the following ways:

- As information that arises before, during, or after a Reiki session
- As a helping presence during a Reiki session
- In dreams and intuition

OTHER TYPES OF GUIDES

You have many other types of spirits that may exist to provide guidance as well, including:

- Sympathetic souls who have been incarnated with you in various lifetimes
- Ancestors
- Members of your soul group
- Ascended masters
- Loved ones who have died
- Your higher self that exists outside of incarnation

Connecting with Your Guides

Connecting with your guides is a matter of asking for guidance and listening. Information from your spirit guides may arrive in the following ways:

- Dreams
- Intuition
- Urges
- Voices of reason
- Words spoken to you through others
- Information provided through psychic insight, channeling, creative flashes, or writing
- Synchronicities
- Leaving objects, such as coins or trinkets

To connect with your guides, all you need to do is ask for guidance and then pay attention to information all around you. Your guides will respond, but it's up to you to pay attention to everything around you to understand that response. When you receive guidance, always act on that guidance and express gratitude.

Using Discernment

Whether working with your spirit guides or communicating with other spirits, it's important that you discern guidance from noise coming from your own mind, your healing partner, or a source that may not have the greatest good as a guiding principle. Ask the following questions to discern whether the information is a form of guidance.

IS THIS MINE?

If you have a physical feeling during a Reiki session ask, "Is this mine?" If the answer is no, act on the physical feeling (move your hands on your healing partner to the position where you're having the feeling in your own body), give thanks for the information, and then visualize the information pushing downward out of your body, through your feet, and into the Earth where it is neutralized.

DOES THIS SERVE THE GREATEST GOOD?

If you believe you are receiving guidance, ask yourself, "Does this information serve the greatest good?" If the information is loving and will do good and not harm, chances are it is guidance. Act on the guidance and give thanks for the information.

Asking Spirits to Leave

Everyone deserves privacy, and it's perfectly fine to set boundaries for receiving guidance or interacting with spirits. To ask a spirit to leave, you can simply say, "Thank you for the information. Please leave now; if you'd like to share more, you can talk to me (set boundary)."

In a few cases dealing with the spirits of people who have died that are trying to communicate, they might be less willing to abide by boundaries, so you can also put up an energetic barrier to keep them away until you're ready to hear their information or guidance. To do this, visualize pushing an energy field from your solar plexus that surrounds you completely. When you're ready to communicate with spirits, you can visualize the barrier retreating into your solar plexus.

A GUIDED MEDITATION TO CONNECT WITH GUIDES

This meditation allows you to do two things: connect with your spirit guides and create an energetic space that can serve as your Reiki healing room.

1. Sit or lie comfortably where you won't be disturbed. Breathe deeply in through your nose and out through your mouth.
2. When you feel relaxed, imagine you are at the end of a street. Notice along the street ahead of you that there are six houses—one in each of the first six chakra colors (red, orange, yellow, green, blue, violet) with a glowing white temple at the other end of the street.
3. Walk down the street, entering each house and pausing within to allow the energy of the house's color to surround you.
4. When you reach the violet house, notice someone waiting at the front door for you. This is your Reiki guide. Enter the house and spend time talking to your guide, asking questions such as how they communicate with you and the types of guidance they provide.
5. When you're ready, thank your Reiki guide and leave the violet house. Walk down the street to the temple.
6. Walk up the temple stairs and enter the temple. Your Reiki guide is standing in the temple next to a healing table surrounded in light. Decorate your temple in any way you wish. Bring into this space any objects you feel you need to support your distance healing efforts while you are here in this temple. You can come here any time to virtually meet your healing partners and your Reiki guides to perform Reiki healing for them. If you like, lie down on the healing table and ask your guide to channel Reiki to you.
7. When you are ready, give thanks to your Reiki guide and exit your temple. Walk down the street again to your starting point, passing all the colorful houses on your way.
8. Now, return your attention to your body once again, noticing your breath as it flows in and out. When you are ready, open your eyes.

The Sacred Significance of Reiki Symbols

Second Degree Reiki has three symbols that perform different functions. There is a fourth symbol you will learn and be attuned to during your Reiki Master-Teacher training and attunement as well. During your attunement, these symbols will either physically or energetically be drawn on your hands to attune you to their energy.

We teach these symbols to help you focus and strengthen your Reiki energy and to allow you to send Reiki through time and space (distance healing). The symbols come from the images Usui Sensei saw in his vision in the cave on Mount Kurama.

In the sections that follow, I will teach you each of the three traditional Usui Ryoho Second Degree Reiki symbols, as well as how to draw and use each of them.

SHOULD REIKI SYMBOLS REMAIN SECRET?

There is a school of thought that suggests Reiki symbols should be secret and never be written down. This teaching came from Mrs. Takata when she was spreading Reiki teachings to the West. It is believed that she wished her students to keep the Reiki symbols secret (and insisted that Reiki remain an oral tradition) to control how Reiki spread out of respect for the practice.

However, today many Reiki Master-Teachers and practitioners do not believe the Reiki symbols need to remain secret because, in order to access them, you must be attuned to them by a Reiki Master-Teacher. In fact, both Usui Sensei and Dr. Hayashi openly shared the symbols in written form in their written materials and teachings.

Therefore, I don't believe the Reiki symbols need to remain secret because both Dr. Hayashi and Usui Sensei shared them freely. It is impossible to misuse the symbols because Reiki always serves the greatest good, and you must be attuned to them to use them. Therefore, there is very little downside to sharing and writing the symbols. Likewise, I believe in sharing the symbols in this book and in my other teachings and works to allow others to access and work with Reiki energy because I believe it is such a powerful and needed tool for healing.

Traditional Second Degree Reiki Symbols

There are three traditional symbols taught and attuned during Second Degree Usui Ryoho Reiki. The three symbols are for physical healing and activation of Second Degree Reiki energy, mental and emotional healing, and spiritual and distance healing. Without these symbols, you are only channeling First Degree Reiki and you will be unable to send the energy across time and distance.

Cho Ku Rei

SYMBOL AND HOW TO DRAW

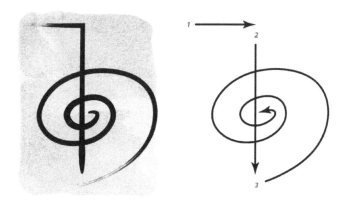

PRONUNCIATION AND ABBREVIATION

Cho ku rei is pronounced "show-koo-ray" or "choh-koo-ray"; abbreviated as CKR.

MEANING

The translation of CKR is "placing all the power of the universe here." CKR is the Reiki power symbol. It activates Second Degree Reiki energy and the other two Second Degree symbols. Therefore, you can either use CKR by itself or before and after the other two Second Degree Reiki symbols to activate them. CKR is also the symbol of physical healing and can help bring energy and balance to issues that are primarily physical (such as a broken leg).

MANTRA

CKR doesn't have a specific mantra, but every time you draw it, activate it by saying its name aloud or in your mind three times.

- Always use it to activate Second Degree Reiki energy by drawing it on your hands before a Reiki session.
- Activate the other two Reiki symbols by drawing a *full Reiki sandwich* in which you draw CKR, the other Reiki symbols, and then CKR again. If using all three symbols, draw CKR + SHK + CKR + HSZN + CKR (see the following sections), saying the name of each symbol aloud or in your head 3 times as you draw it.

Other times to use CKR:

- To help break physical habits or creations
- To dissipate dis-ease or negative physical patterns
- To stop progressions that don't serve you
- To change the energy of a physical space (such as drawing it in the four corners of your healing space to invite Reiki in before a session)
- To provide a protective barrier in a space
- To cleanse objects
- To energize food or drink with Reiki before you consume it
- To energize plants or water given to plants

ALTERNATE VERSIONS

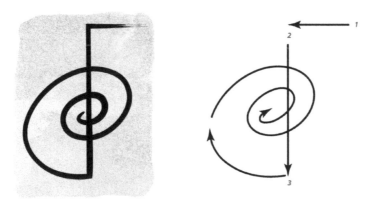

Some people use reverse CKR to close their Reiki sandwich because they believe it brings energetic balance.

Sei He Ki

SYMBOL AND HOW TO DRAW

 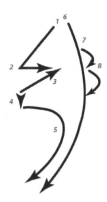

PRONUNCIATION AND ABBREVIATION

Sei he ki is pronounced "say-hay-key"; abbreviated SHK.

MEANING

SHK means "God and man become one." SHK is the emotional and mental energy healing symbol.

MANTRA

SHK doesn't have a specific mantra. Every time you draw it, activate it by saying its name aloud or in your mind three times.

WHEN TO USE

When drawing SHK, activate it by surrounding it with CKR so CKR + SHK + CKR. This is called the *SHK sandwich*. There are many times to use SHK to help clear emotional blockages:

- To release energetic blockages and resistance caused by unsuppressed emotions
- To release addictions
- To resolve long-term emotional problems
- To remove obstacles
- To help resolve relationship issues
- To process negative emotions

- To process grief
- To enhance affirmations
- To improve emotional intelligence
- To improve memory
- To spark intuition
- To calm emotionally charged situations
- To improve communication
- To spark creativity
- To help find lost items

Hon Sha Ze Sho Nen

SYMBOL AND HOW TO DRAW

 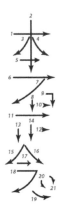

PRONUNCIATION AND ABBREVIATION

Hon Sha Ze Sho Nen is pronounced "On-SHAW-ze-SHOW-nen"; abbreviated HSZN.

MEANING

HSZN means, "no past, no present, no future." It is the symbol of the spiritual realm and the Reiki distance healing symbol. To send Reiki across time or distance, you must use HSZN and activate it with CKR, which is often called the *HSZN sandwich*: CKR + HSZN + CKR.

MANTRA

HSZN doesn't have a specific mantra. Every time you draw it, activate it by saying its name aloud or in your mind three times.

WHEN TO USE

- Any time you wish to send Reiki across a distance of time or space
- To work with deep-seated issues
- To send Reiki to large groups or situations
- To shorten the length of a Reiki session
- To help bring insight and clarity to spiritual issues

Nontraditional Reiki Symbols

There are also several nontraditional Reiki symbols that come from other Reiki systems such as Karuna Ki Reiki (Mother Earth Reiki). Some practitioners use these symbols to increase the specificity of their treatments. I seldom use them because I like to allow the Reiki energy to flow in the way that serves the greatest good, and I feel being too specific in my intention may limit the ways in which Reiki energy can bring about healing. However, I want you to be aware of these symbols and their uses if you'd like to use them in your own practice.

Zonar

SYMBOL AND HOW TO DRAW

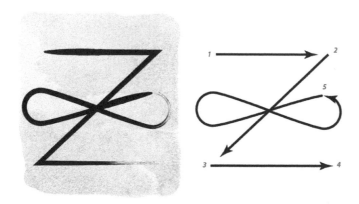

Zonar represents the infinite or eternal. It is good for working with karmic issues from past lives.

Harth

SYMBOL AND HOW TO DRAW

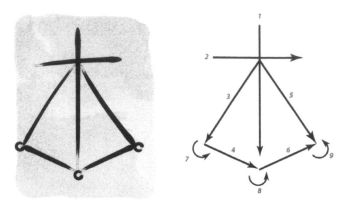

Harth is the symbol of truth, harmony, and love. It can reverse negativity and bring love into situations. It also opens a channel to guidance from higher realms, such as guides or your higher self.

Fire Dragon

SYMBOL AND HOW TO DRAW

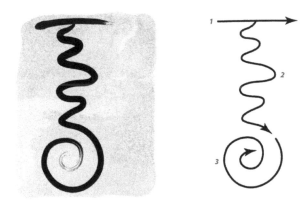

Fire Dragon represents the energy traveling through your chakras. You can draw it in either direction (down or up) to move energy in the desired direction.

Johrei

SYMBOL AND HOW TO DRAW

Johrei, a symbol of white light, is used to stimulate healing and release blockages. It's also a symbol to use to cleanse spaces or protect them.

Dumo

SYMBOL AND HOW TO DRAW

Some Reiki Masters use *dumo* during Reiki attunements.

Incorporating Reiki Symbols Into Treatments

I incorporate symbols into my treatments intuitively, and I use them at specific times, such as when I wish to channel Second Degree Reiki or send distance healing. Always use at least CKR and draw it onto your hands at the beginning of a session to activate Second Degree Reiki energy, and always use the HSZN sandwich (CKR + HSZN + CKR) or the full Reiki sandwich (CKR + SHK + CKR + HSZN + CKR) before sending distance energy.

Other times you can incorporate the symbols into treatments include:

◆ If you are working with blocked mental, spiritual, physical, or emotional energy to release blockages

◆ To empower a specific intention you've set with your healing partner

◆ When you send Reiki to a situation or to a large group of people (page 124)

◆ When you send Reiki back or forward through time (page 124)

◆ Any time you feel intuitively guided to do so

There are a number of ways you can bring the symbols into your practice:

◆ Draw them on your hands with a finger at the beginning of a session.

◆ Draw them on your healing partner's body. Any time you do this, tap the symbols into the body with 3 taps of the forefinger and middle finger on your dominant hand, which is your *giving hand*.

◆ Visualize them and then project that visualization into your hands or into your healing partner's body.

◆ Draw them on a piece of paper with your healing partner's name or on a photograph to send distant healing.

In the next chapter, you will learn more about using the symbols as part of your practice of Second Degree Reiki.

CHAPTER SIX

Second Degree Reiki Healing Techniques

When working with Second Degree Reiki, you could simply draw CKR on your palms to let the Second Degree Reiki flow and use the techniques and hand positions you learned in First Degree Reiki (page 62). However, with many new tools available to you as a Second Degree Reiki practitioner, now is the time to learn and grow in your healing practices. In this chapter you'll learn an array of techniques for distance healing and incorporating additional modalities into your work as a Reiki practitioner.

Preparing for Treatment Sessions

In Second Degree Reiki, you are invited to work with the three pillars of Reiki to help intuitively guide you during treatment. Second Degree teaches simple preparedness techniques to invite intuitive information through the practice of the three pillars of Reiki.

Pillar 1: Gassho

You've already learned about Gassho in chapter 2 (page 27), and it is the first pillar of Reiki you use to prepare for a Reiki session. Begin your session standing with your hands in Gassho to clear your mind. Likewise, return to Gassho at any point during your session to ask for more intuitive information to come to you if you need it.

Pillar 2: Reiji-Ho

The second pillar of Reiki is *Reiji-ho* ("ray-jee-HOH"). This is where you invite the Second Degree Reiki and ask for intuitive information. To perform Reiji-ho:

1. Stand at your healing partner's head with your hands in Gassho and your eyes closed.

2. Mentally draw the full Reiki sandwich (CKR + SHK + CKR + HSZN + CKR) and ask for Reiki to flow.

3. As you draw the symbols, say the name of each 3 times.

4. Ask Reiki energy to balance your subject.

5. Keeping your hands in Gassho, move them to your third eye chakra and ask them to guide you to where energy is needed.

6. Now, without any personal agenda or desires, allow this to guide your hands.

Pillar 3: Chiryo

Chiryo ("chi-RYE-oh") means treatment. This is where you allow the information you've received during your preparations of Gassho and Reiji-ho to guide you in your healing partner's treatment. To perform Chiryo:

1. Hold your hands where you are guided for three to five minutes, or until you feel intuitively guided to move.

2. Return to Gassho. Ask to be guided again and move where your intuition tells you to place your hands.

3. Continue this until you are guided that the session is complete.

Integrating Crystals, Essential Oils, and Other Tools

If you are drawn to other forms of energy healing, you can also incorporate these modalities into your Reiki session. Although additional tools aren't necessary, they can help create a healing environment, strengthen your own intuition, and work synergistically with the Second Degree Reiki energy to provide a more powerful and directed healing session.

So, how do you decide which other tools you could or should use during an energy session? Here are some criteria to consider:

◆ What are you intuitively guided to work with? Listen to this intuition.

◆ Has your healing partner requested anything specific? If they have and you have the capacity to use that tool, then bring it into the session.

◆ Crystals are always easy to incorporate into a session because merely having them in your space can refine the energy. If you feel drawn to place a certain crystal on or near your healing partner, do this.

◆ Diffuse essential oils in sessions unless your healing partner has a sensitivity to fragrance. Don't use essential oils directly on your healing partner's skin or body unless you have studied their properties and understand how to use them.

◆ Sound is also something that you use naturally in an energy healing session, as the music or Reiki timer you select can add to meditative practices. Choose music that is relaxing and made for meditation. If you are aware your healing partner has issues with a specific chakra, you can also choose music or sound that balances that chakra, such as a solfeggio or a singing bowl with the right pitch to balance the energy of that specific chakra.

Hands-On Treatment with Symbols

Even though you can now do distant healing, whenever possible, I recommend working with your healing partners hands-on and in-person. There is no substitute for this personal contact, and it allows you to interact with and observe your healing partner in order to make in-the-moment intuitive decisions based on your healing partner's shifting energetic conditions during their session.

Hand Scanning

One way to determine where your healing partner needs the most energy balancing is by *hand scanning*. With hand scanning, you move your *receiving hand* (nondominant hand) through your healing partner's energy (auric) field along the line of the chakras. This allows you to feel imbalances in your healing partner's energy in both the auras and the chakras.

To scan your healing partner's energetic field:

1. Ask your healing partner to lie on their back.

2. Stand at your healing partner's head. Draw CKR on both palms (or the full Reiki sandwich) and hold them in Gassho until you feel the energy flow.

3. Take your nondominant hand, which is your receiving hand, and hold it about 2 inches above your healing partner's crown chakra.

4. Now, working from crown to toes, move your hand slowly down the midline of your healing partner's body, maintaining a distance of about 2 inches from their body.

5. As you move your hand, pay attention to shifts in sensation in your palm; you may notice hot, cold, tingling, pushes, numbness, or pulling. And although these signals may mean different things to different practitioners, when you experience the sensations, it informs you there is a disturbance in your healing partner's energetic field in that location, so you may want to return to that location during your session to channel energy.

6. Return to the crown chakra. Repeat the scan, this time moving down each side of the body (right arm and leg, left arm and leg) from their head to their toes.

Self-Treatment

Remember that if you wish to channel Second Degree Reiki energy, you must use CKR to activate it.

◆ Draw CKR on both of your palms and invite the energy to flow. Then, complete a hands-on self-treatment as outlined in chapter 3 (page 47).

- Draw any of the symbols on areas of your body where you have dis-ease or energetic imbalance. Be sure to tap the symbols 3 times and repeat their names 3 times as you draw them.

- Balance the hara line chakras by drawing the full Reiki sandwich (CKR + SHK + CKR + HSZN + CKR) on your root chakra and on your crown chakra. Then, hold one hand on your crown chakra and one on your root chakra and visualize the energy flowing between your hands along the hara line through each chakra.

Healing Partner Treatment

There are a number of ways you can work with the Reiki symbols during hands-on treatment with a healing partner. Begin by inviting the Second Degree energy to flow by drawing CKR on your palms and standing with your hands in Gassho until you feel the energy flow. Do this at the beginning of every hands-on Reiki session. Other ways to use the symbols during treatment:

- Draw the symbols on your healing partner's body, and then lightly tap the symbol in 3 times. When you draw the symbol, repeat its name in your head 3 times.

- Draw the full Reiki sandwich and visualize sending Reiki to your healing partner's past self while channeling Reiki through your hands to them at the same time to help heal deep karmic issues.

- If your healing partner has shared an affirmation or intention for the session in their initial consultation, write it on a slip of paper and draw the full Reiki sandwich on the paper. Have your healing partner hold the paper during the session as you channel Reiki to them.

- Help your healing partner to continue to experience the bliss they feel after a Reiki session. Using a finger, draw the full Reiki sandwich on a clear quartz crystal before the session and have your healing partner hold it in their *giving hand* (dominant hand) during the Reiki session while visualizing the energy and good feelings from the session flowing into the crystal. They can keep the crystal with them and hold it in their receiving (nondominant) hand when they want to recapture that feeling after their session.

Reiki Symbols for Daily Life

You can also use the Reiki symbols to bring more Reiki energy into your activities of daily living. In this way, Reiki becomes a lifestyle that always invites the manifestation of the most positive form of universal energy.

Working with Plants, Animals, and Objects

I encourage you to make Reiki a daily practice. Inviting Reiki energy into every aspect of your life can help you to experience the highest expression of plants, animals, and objects as well as how the energy of these things manifests in your life.

KEEP YOUR VEHICLE IN WORKING ORDER

Keep your car serviceable and in good energetic shape by doing the following:

1. With your finger, draw CKR on the steering wheel before you drive anywhere.

2. As you do, repeat the name CKR 3 times and visualize white light energy flowing through your car and forming a protective bubble around it.

CHANNEL VITAL ENERGY TO YOUR PLANTS

Give your plants an energetic boost with Reiki.

1. Fill a watering can with water.

2. With your finger, draw CKR on the outside of the watering can.

3. Use this to water your plants.

MORE REIKI SYMBOLS FOR PLANTS, ANIMALS, AND OBJECTS

Additionally, try the following:

◆ With your finger, draw CKR or the full Reiki sandwich on objects you give as gifts to energize them with Reiki energy and positive intent.
◆ With your finger, draw CKR on electronics before you fire them up for the day.

◆ Send distance Reiki energy to injured wild animals or pets you can't touch by drawing the full Reiki sandwich on your hands with your finger and visualizing that animal between the palms of your hands.

◆ If you've lost an item, visualize the item and then visualize a SHK Reiki sandwich drawn on the item (CKR + SHK + CKR). Now, in your mind's eye, zoom out from the item and see if you can picture in your mind's eye where it is located.

Working with Ideas and Concepts

SHK is the symbol of the mental realm, making it an excellent symbol to use when working with ideas and concepts. It can help stimulate your mental acuity and responses as well as sparking intuition and creativity. Remember that when you work with SHK, you should always activate it with CKR so it is a SHK sandwich (CKR + SHK + CKR).

◆ If you're studying for a test or trying to understand a difficult concept, with your finger or mentally, draw the SHK sandwich on your study materials.

◆ With a pen or pencil, draw a SHK sandwich on written affirmations to help charge them with intention.

◆ If you are an artist, either draw the SHK sandwich into the base layer of your design (you can paint or draw over it) or draw it with a finger on your blank canvas to spark intuition during your session.

◆ With your finger, a pen, or a pencil, draw the SHK sandwich in your journal at the beginning of a journaling session to spark insight as you write.

For Cleansing Negative Energy

One of the best ways to cleanse negative energy is to displace it with a positive energy such as Reiki. Use the Reiki symbols to invite Reiki energy in to displace negativity in multiple aspects of your life.

CLEANSE SPACES

Cleanse negativity from spaces and invite positive energy in by using the CKR symbol.

1. Starting at the front door, with a finger, draw CKR over every opening into the space—doors, windows, fireplaces, drains—as well as all corners of the space.

2. Move clockwise throughout the space doing this until you have completed the circuit.

CLEANSE NEGATIVE ENERGY AT WORK

If you work near a coworker who has lots of negative energy or your workspace has negativity:

1. Use a pen or pencil to draw CKR on a piece of paper.

2. Place it somewhere in your space (or tape it to the bottom of your chair) to absorb the negativity.

MORE IDEAS FOR USING REIKI SYMBOLS TO CLEANSE NEGATIVITY

Additionally, try the following:

◆ With a finger, draw CKR on used or antique items you bring into your home to cleanse them of the energy of where they were before.
◆ Cleanse food and drink of any negativity and invite healthy, positive energy by drawing CKR with your finger over the top of any food or beverages before you consume them.
◆ Cleanse crystals and other objects by placing them in a bowl and drawing the full Reiki sandwich over the top of the bowl or on the bowl's surface with your finger.

For Protecting Self and Others

Using the Reiki symbols can also help provide personal protection by creating a protective barrier of positive Reiki energy around you to keep negativity at bay.

◆ Carry a piece of paper with the full Reiki sandwich written on it in your pocket.
◆ Visualize the full Reiki sandwich on your solar plexus, and then visualize a bubble of Reiki energy expanding out from your solar plexus to surround you, your family, and your entire home.

- Place a slip of paper with the full Reiki sandwich written on it in your child's jacket, lunchbox, or another item they keep with them when they go to school.
- Draw the full Reiki sandwich on items of clothing or jewelry you or your loved ones wear to provide Reiki energy protection throughout the day.
- With your finger, draw the full Reiki sandwich on a clear quartz or black tourmaline crystal and keep it with you in a pocket to provide Reiki protection throughout the day.

To Change Habits and Behaviors

Use various Reiki symbols to help bring needed change to bad habits and behaviors. If the habit is purely physical, you can use CKR. If the habit also has a mental and emotional aspect to it, you can use the SHK sandwich. If it's a deeply ingrained habit or behavior, use the full Reiki sandwich.

CHANGE A HABIT WHEN IT FORMS

Send distant healing to yourself or your healing partner to the period when a specific behavior or habit was formed. You do not need to know the specific period or incident; your intention that the Reiki energy go to this time and this habit is all that is needed. To do this:

1. Write a description of the habit on a slip of paper and then fold it.

2. Write the full Reiki sandwich on the paper.

3. With your finger, draw the full Reiki sandwich on your hands and hold the paper between your hands.

4. In your mind, state your intention to send the energy to when the habit was originally formed.

BREAK HABITS WITH A PSYCHOLOGICAL BASIS

Use the SHK sandwich to address habits that have a psychological basis, such as addiction.

1. Write the name of the habit on a piece of paper (as well as the healing partner's name, if you're sending Reiki energy for them) and then fold it.

2. Write the SHK sandwich on the paper.

3. With your finger, draw the full Reiki sandwich on your hands and channel Reiki to the paper with the intention of removing the blockages and shifting the energy contributing to the behavior.

To Heal Relationships and Emotional Issues

SHK is the symbol of emotional healing, so it is an especially helpful symbol to use when you're working to heal emotional or relationship issues.

HEAL YOUR RELATIONSHIP

When attempting to heal a relationship, it's important that you don't have an agenda other than bringing about loving healing that serves the greatest good of both parties. To bring about healing:

1. Use a picture of both parties in the relationship or write both of their names on a piece of paper.

2. Write the SHK sandwich on the photo or paper.

3. With your finger, draw the full Reiki sandwich on both hands.

4. Hold the paper or photo between both hands and channel Reiki to it with the intention of serving the greatest good of both parties.

HEAL EMOTIONAL ISSUES

If you understand the emotional basis behind an issue, you can use the SHK sandwich to channel Reiki energy to help resolve the emotions associated with the issue.

1. Determine the chakra location associated with the emotional issue (see chakras in chapter 1).

2. With your finger, draw the SHK sandwich on the affected chakra and tap it 3 times.

3. With your finger, draw the full Reiki sandwich on both palms and channel Reiki energy to that chakra until you feel a release, or until you feel guided to move your hands.

Sending Reiki into the Past and the Future

In ultimate reality, there is no time or space. Time and space are constructs we work with in our embodied (human) state to have the fully human experience. However, because there is no time or space outside of the three dimensions we live in as embodied humans, you can easily send Reiki to the past or the future just as you would send it across distance. To do this:

1. Determine the period, time, or event to which you will send Reiki.

2. Write a description of the person, place, time, or event in the past or future on a piece of paper and write the full Reiki sandwich on the paper.

3. With your finger, draw the full Reiki sandwich on each of your palms.

4. Hold the paper between your hands and channel energy to it until you feel compelled to stop.

5. You can also intend for the Reiki to last for a certain period (such as an hour, a day, etc.). To do this, as you channel the Reiki, state your intention in your mind for how long the energy will continue to channel to that person, place, time, or event.

Distance Treatments

Although I prefer hands-on healing, sometimes because of constraints of time, space, distance, or circumstance, working with a healing partner hands-on is not possible. Fortunately, there are many methods for sending Reiki at a distance that are as powerful as working with a healing partner hands-on. Therefore, learning methods for providing distance treatments is an essential part of Second Degree Reiki.

Ethics and Consent

Ethics are an essential part of any energy healing practice, including Reiki. When you do energy work, you must always do so from a place of integrity.

It's important as an energy healing practitioner, if you are working with healing partners, that you decide what your values and ethics are surrounding your practice of energy healing. Some ethics are required by law, such as having the appropriate licensing/certification in place, following ethical business practices, keeping appropriate documentation, and adhering to the Health Insurance Portability and Accountability Act (HIPAA), but others are deeply personal.

Likewise, within the framework of Reiki, we are offered a simple set of ethical standards through the five principles of Reiki (page 25).

One ethic all Reiki practitioners should adhere to is consent: Always seek consent when channeling Reiki either at a distance or in-person. In-person, of course, you simply ask, but what should you do at a distance?

◆ Seek verbal or written consent first. If you do not receive consent, do not send Reiki.

◆ If you are unable to ask (such as during an emergency or when working with an animal), see if you can obtain energetic consent. In your mind's eye, ask for consent and see if you feel a sense of allowing or a sense of blocking and act within that framework.

◆ If you are still unsure whether you have received consent, channel distance Reiki with the intention it goes to your intended subject if they consent to it, and if they don't, it goes to where it serves the greatest good.

How It Works

In quantum physics, there is a proven principle called *entanglement*, something Einstein referred to as "spooky action at a distance." When particles of matter have been energetically entangled, they remain entangled forever, and any force applied to one of the entangled particles affects the other particle regardless of how far apart the two particles are separated by time and space. Because all matter was entangled at the Big Bang, that means everything is connected to everything else. This is how you are able to send Reiki energy across time and space.

Sending distance Reiki works through intention. Using the Reiki distance symbols is one part of stating your intention to send Reiki energy to a specific person, place, and time for a specific period. Along with the intention stated by using the Reiki distance symbols either as a full Reiki sandwich or a HSZN sandwich, you should also state your intent either in your mind or by writing it down. For example, "I intend to channel Second Degree Reiki energy to Bob Smith at 411 Main Street in Jonesboro, Arkansas, to serve his greatest good."

Techniques for Distance Healing

There are numerous techniques you can use for distance healing. Feel free to adapt the techniques as you are intuitively guided to do so. Intention is the key to sending distance Reiki—the mechanics supply a form for sending Reiki across time and space to provide you the freedom to do so in the manner that makes the most sense to you. Always end the session by running your hands under cool water to break the energetic connection.

Surrogate Method

The surrogate method is the most similar to a hands-on Reiki session. In the surrogate method, you use a doll or stuffed animal as a stand-in for your healing partner.

1. State your intention for the surrogate to be a stand-in for your healing partner, such as "I intend this stuffed bear to be an energetic surrogate for Bob Smith in Jonesboro, Arkansas."

2. Use a finger to draw the full Reiki sandwich on both of your hands.

3. Provide a full Reiki session to your surrogate using the hand positions or an intuitive session.

Photograph Method

You can also work with a photograph of your healing partner.

1. Write the full Reiki sandwich onto the photograph (either with your finger or with a pen or pencil).

2. Hold the photo between your hands and channel Reiki to the photograph until you feel drawn to stop.

Piece of Paper Method

In the absence of a photograph, write the person's identifying information (such as name and address) on a piece of paper, and then channel Reiki to it as you would in the Photograph Method.

Small Surrogate Method

Designate a small object, such as a crystal, as a stand in for your healing partner by stating your intention, "This crystal will serve as an energetic stand-in for (your healing partner's name)."

1. With your finger, draw the full Reiki sandwich on the small surrogate.

2. With your finger, draw the full Reiki sandwich on both of your hands.

3. Hold the small surrogate between your hands and channel Reiki energy to it until you feel guided to stop.

Mini Me Method

If you are channeling Reiki to someone whose energy you are very familiar with, such as a close friend or family member or pet, you can use this method.

1. Use a finger to draw the full Reiki sandwich on each of your hands.

2. Cup your hands together and visualize your healing partner between them, receiving the energy.

3. Continue channeling the Reiki until you feel guided to stop.

Distance Healing Room

You can also energetically meet your healing partner in a distance healing room. Use the guided meditation on page 119 to set up your distance healing room. To work with a healing partner in your distance healing room:

1. Sit or lie comfortably with your eyes closed.

2. Draw the full Reiki sandwich on both hands.

3. Practice Gassho meditation until you feel calm and relaxed. Then, visualize your distance healing room.

4. See your healing partner entering the room and lying down on your healing table.

5. Perform a Reiki session in your mind's eye either using an intuitive session or the hand positions.

Group and Situational Healing

You can also send Reiki healing to groups and situations. To do this:

1. On a piece of paper, write a description of the situation or the names of the people to whom you'll be channeling Reiki.

2. Fold the paper and write the full Reiki sandwich on the outside.

3. With your finger, draw the full Reiki sandwich on both hands.

4. Hold the paper between your hands and channel Reiki energy to it.

5. As you channel the Reiki energy, state the intention to send the Reiki to those people, places, and circumstances written on the piece of paper if it serves the greatest good and/or you have consent to do so. If it doesn't serve the greatest good or you don't have consent, ask for the Reiki energy to go where it serves the highest good.

6. Channel the energy until you feel guided to stop.

7. Give thanks for the energy and reaffirm that it goes to serve the greatest good.

Reiki Box

Use a *Reiki box* to send energy to large groups of people. Write the names of the people you will send Reiki to on slips of paper and place them in your Reiki box. Then, use your finger to draw the full Reiki sandwich on both hands and hold the box between your hands. Channel Reiki energy to the box until you feel guided to stop.

Your Reiki box can be anything. Use any lidded container that you are drawn to, such as a wooden box, a decorated cardboard box, or a trinket box. A few things you need to avoid with a Reiki box:

♦   Avoid metal boxes, which will reflect the Reiki energy instead of absorbing it.

♦   Avoid boxes with black or red crystals on the outside, as those crystals are protective and could keep the Reiki energy from entering the box.

Programming Future or Repeat Treatments

You can also "program" future or repeat treatments. This is a great way to make sure someone receives Reiki in the moment they need it, regardless of whether you're available at that exact time.

You can also use this method to set repeating treatments—for example, for someone who has a series of events where they want Reiki while the event is occurring. I've done this with a healing partner receiving chemotherapy treatments, so she would receive Reiki even if I wasn't available during each of her treatments. To do this:

1. On a piece of paper, write the person's name and the dates, times, and durations for each Reiki treatment. For example, "Jason Whittaker, Wednesday June 3, 2020, from 9:30 a.m. to 11:30 p.m. before and during his French final." Or "Jill Jones of Seattle for 30 minutes before extending to 30 minutes after each chemotherapy appointment for her breast cancer." If you have specific dates and times, use them. Otherwise, simply write when the Reiki is intended to flow, why, and the duration.

2. Fold the piece of paper and write the full Reiki sandwich on it.

3. Draw with your finger the full Reiki sandwich on each of your palms.

4. Hold the paper between your palms and channel Reiki to it until you feel guided to stop. As you channel, if you wish you can restate the name of the person and your intention for where, when, how long, and how frequently it flows in your mind's eye.

CHAPTER SEVEN

Reiki Sequences for Emotional Well-Being and Spiritual Awakening

The following 10 sequences can help create vibrational changes to bring about healing for emotional well-being and spiritual awakening. Reiki treatment is only part of the story; these sequences can help rebalance energy that may be preventing emotional and spiritual growth, but your healing partner also must be willing to do the emotional and spiritual work and engage in practices on their own time that support these energetic changes. For each of the sequences, if you've been attuned to Second Degree Reiki, draw the full Reiki sandwich on both of your hands. If you are a First Degree Reiki practitioner, you can still use the sequence, but you will use only the hand positions and skip the steps where you work with symbols. Hold each hand position for three minutes, or until you sense release.

Abundance Consciousness

The issue my healing partners are most likely to ask me about is abundance or prosperity. And although it may seem that these issues are circumstantial, in fact, they are spiritual and emotional issues associated with your consciousness and where you place your focus. It's important to understand that prosperity and abundance aren't necessarily about having enough money (although that can certainly be a part of it), but rather are about bringing an abundance of the things that matter into your life, such as friends, family, joy, and more.

Affected Chakras

▶ Third eye
▶ Throat
▶ Solar plexus
▶ Sacral

Step-by-Step Instructions

1. Stand at your healing partner's side. Place your hands on the Hara.

2. Place your hands in the Navel hand position.

3. Place your hands in the Solar Plexus hand position.

4. Place your hands in the Throat hand position.

5. Move to your healing partner's head. Place your hands in the following sequence: Back of Head – Ears – Eyes.

6. Return to your healing partner's side. Place your dominant hand on your healing partner's third eye chakra and place your nondominant hand on the solar plexus chakra. Visualize the energy flowing between your hands.

Tip: On a piece of paper, write the affirmation, "I give thanks to the universe that I have an abundance of all things I desire and need in my life." Fold the paper and write the full Reiki sandwich on it. Have your healing partner hold this in their receiving (nondominant) hand through the Reiki session.

Compassion

Compassion is the human manifestation of love. It allows us to step outside our own experience and into someone else's so we can proceed with love in the way we think of them, communicate with them, and interact with them. Cultivating compassion is one of the most important qualities we can create as embodied spirits because it allows us to approach others with kindness and care.

Affected Chakras

- Throat
- Heart
- Solar plexus

Step-by-Step Instructions

1. Stand at your healing partner's side. Place one hand on their solar plexus chakra and one on their heart chakra in a bridge position. Visualize the energy flowing between your hands and through their heart.

2. If you practice Second Degree Reiki, draw the full Reiki sandwich on your healing partner's heart chakra and tap it in 3 times with the forefinger and middle finger of your dominant hand.

3. Hold the Heart hand position, visualizing pink energy flowing from your hands and into their heart.

Tip: As you channel Reiki to your healing partner, repeat the Buddhist mantra "Om mane padme hum" (pronounced "ohm mahnee pad may hoom"). This mantra helps cycle energy from the mind to the heart, which can spark compassion and understanding.

Creativity

One of the purposes of souls incarnating as humans is to create, and many believe that our primary purpose as incarnated souls is to create our own reality in ways that serve the greatest good of the universe. Creative ideation is born in the sacral chakra and expressed via the throat chakra. Therefore, balance between these two chakras is essential for living creatively fulfilled lives.

Affected Chakras

- Throat
- Heart
- Solar plexus
- Sacral

Step-by-Step Instructions

1. Stand at your healing partner's side. If you practice Second Degree Reiki, draw the SHK sandwich over your healing partner's sacral chakra and tap it in 3 times with the forefinger and middle finger of your dominant hand.

2. Place your hands in the Hara hand position. Visualize orange light streaming from your hands into your healing partner's root chakra.

3. Place your hands in the Navel hand position.

4. Place your hands in the Solar Plexus hand position.

5. Place your hands in the Heart hand position.

6. For Second Degree practitioners, draw the SHK sandwich over your healing partner's throat chakra and tap it in 3 times with the forefinger and middle finger of your dominant hand.

7. Hold the Throat hand position. Visualize blue light streaming from your hands and into your healing partner's throat chakra.

Continued

8. Move your dominant hand to your healing partner's Hara. Hold this bridge position, visualizing energy flowing from Hara to Throat in an unimpeded flow.

Tip: Place a creativity crystal grid under the healing table. Use a simple circle. In the center of the circle, place a blue stone such as blue calcite, celestite, or aquamarine. In a circle around the center stone, place 4 to 8 pieces of carnelian.

Forgiveness

Whether it is forgiveness of self or others, this is an important first step in personal and spiritual growth. We get hurt throughout our lives. Sometimes, we hurt ourselves or make what we feel are stupid, unforgiveable mistakes that change what we believe should be the course of our lives. However, to move forward as a fully functioning and emotionally and spiritually healthy being, we must release anger, hurt, and disillusionment we hold toward ourselves or others out of the mistaken belief that something shouldn't have happened. To go on believing something shouldn't have occurred is merely arguing with reality and generating lower vibrational energy that blocks us from living to our full potential. Forgiveness is ultimately an act that is about compassion for self. When you forgive someone, you're not saying, "It's okay that you did this." Instead, you're acknowledging that, although it happened, you are choosing to no longer let it affect your own life.

Affected Chakras

▶ Throat
▶ Heart
▶ Solar plexus

Step-by-Step Instructions

1. Ask your healing partner to close their eyes and visualize the person they need to forgive. Tell them that as you channel Reiki, they should visualize the energetic ties connecting them to the other person and see themselves cutting those ties as they repeat the mantras "forgive" and "release."

2. Stand at your healing partner's side. Second Degree practitioners draw the SHK sandwich (CKR + SHK + CKR) on your healing partner's solar plexus chakra and tap it in 3 times with the forefinger and middle finger of your dominant hand.

Continued

3. Place your hands in the Solar Plexus hand position. Visualize golden light streaming from your hands into your healing partner's solar plexus chakra.

4. With your finger, draw the full Reiki sandwich on your healing partner's heart chakra and tap it in 3 times with the forefinger and middle finger of your dominant hand.

5. Place your hands in the Heart hand position. Visualize pink light streaming from your hands into your healing partner's heart chakra.

6. Place your hands in the Throat hand position. Visualize blue light streaming from your hands into your healing partner's throat chakra.

Tip: Rhodochrosite is a crystal that generates the energy of forgiveness. Place a freshly cleansed piece of rhodochrosite on your healing partner's heart chakra throughout the treatment. Channel Reiki energy directly through the crystal when you come to the heart chakra.

Healing the Past

Although our spirits live in the Eternal Moment of Now, our bodies and minds perceive movement through the illusion of space-time as reality. In moving through space-time, we often carry the baggage of our past along with us in the form of conditioning, hurt, pain, and trauma. This Reiki sequence can help release the hold the past has over us so we can move forward with present-time focus.

Affected Chakras

▸ Solar plexus
▸ Sacral
▸ Root

Step-by-Step Instructions

1. Stand at your healing partner's side. Draw the SHK sandwich over your healing partner's root chakra and tap it in 3 times with the forefinger and middle finger of your dominant hand.

2. Place your hands in the Groin hand position. Visualize red light streaming from your hands into your healing partner's root chakra.

3. Place your hands in the Hara position. Visualize reddish-orange light streaming from your hands into your healing partner's hara.

4. Draw the SHK sandwich over your healing partner's navel and tap it in 3 times with the forefinger and middle finger of your dominant hand.

5. Place your hands in the Navel hand position. Visualize orange light streaming from your hands into your healing partner's sacral chakra.

6. Draw the SHK sandwich over your healing partner's solar plexus chakra and tap it in 3 times with the forefinger and middle finger of your dominant hand.

Continued

7. Place your hands in the Solar Plexus hand position.

8. At the end of the session, have your healing partner sit up. Sweep their aura from head to feet, touching the floor to ground the energy. As you do, visualize pulling all the energy you released downward out of the aura and into the Earth.

Tip: Suggest that, during the Reiki session, your healing partner visualizes hurts from the past as dark shadows in their energy field and then sees those dark shadows dissipate in the light as the Reiki energy permeates them.

Healthy Sexuality

An unhealthy sense of self as a sexual being is primarily a sacral chakra function, but a number of issues that arise throughout our lives can contribute, such as social and religious conditioning and messages, negative sexual experiences, and deficits of self-love and self-esteem. Therefore, although working with the solar plexus is the primary way to strengthen and clarify sexual identity and healthy sexuality, you also need to energetically work with the multifaceted emotional, social, and physical causes that can affect it.

Affected Chakras

- ▶ Solar plexus
- ▶ Sacral
- ▶ Root

Step-by-Step Instructions

1. Stand at your healing partner's side. Draw CKR over your healing partner's root chakra and tap it in 3 times with the forefinger and middle finger of your dominant hand.

2. Place your hands in the Groin hand position.

3. Keep your dominant hand in the Groin hand position and move your other hand to the Hara.

4. Move your dominant hand to the Hara so both hands are in this position.

5. Move your nondominant hand to the Navel hand position, holding your other hand in the Hara position still.

6. Move your dominant hand to the Navel hand position so both hands are in the Navel position.

7. Move your nondominant hand to the Solar Plexus hand position, holding your other hand in the Navel position still.

Continued

8. Move both hands to the Solar Plexus hand position.

9. Keeping your dominant hand on the Solar Plexus hand position, move your other hand to the Groin hand position.

10. Move both hands back to the Groin hand position. Hovering your hands, sweep upward from groin to heart. Visualize pulling the energy from groin to heart as you do this to bring this physical energy into the loving presence of heart energy.

Tip: For people who have deeply rooted issues associated with sexual or gender identity, or for those who have had traumatic sexual experiences in their past, recommend talk therapy with a qualified professional to help them process their complex feelings about this issue. Talk therapy can be a very supportive modality to assist with deep-seated emotional and spiritual issues.

Karmic Healing

Your karma is a set of challenges and issues you come into each life-time with. Karma isn't punishment; rather, it is a set of circumstances, challenges, personality traits, and relationships that you agree to work with in this lifetime in order to become a more well-rounded soul. This sequence for karmic healing is to help us understand and work with the karmic issues we deal with—not to make them go away.

Affected Chakras

▸ Crown
▸ Root

Step-by-Step Instructions

1. Stand at your healing partner's head. Place your hands in the Eyes hand position.

2. Place your hands in the Ears hand position.

3. Place your hands in the Back of the Head hand position.

4. Move to your healing partner's side and place your hands in the Groin hand position.

5. Move your dominant (giving) hand back to the crown of your healing partner's head while holding your nondominant (receiving) hand in the Groin hand position. Visualize energy flowing between your hands.

Tip: Have your healing partner hold a piece of snowflake obsidian in their non-dominant hand during their session. This crystal connects root chakra energy to crown chakra energy to help bring enlightenment and understanding of karmic issues.

Oneness

Oneness is the understanding of your connection to All That Is. It is the connectedness of you in your physically embodied state to Source energy, which is the energy everyone and everything came from and will return to after the experience of physical embodiment is complete. Whether you recognize it, you are part of the Oneness even in your physically embodied state, but you have come with filters in place that cause you to experience yourself as a separate being. Awareness of the Oneness while still recognizing yourself as an embodied individual can lead to spiritual growth.

Affected Chakras

- ▸ Crown
- ▸ Solar plexus
- ▸ Root

Step-by-Step Instructions

1. Stand at your healing partner's feet and hold your hands in the following sequence of hand positions: Feet – Ankles – Knees.

2. Move to your healing partner's side. Draw the full Reiki sandwich over their root chakra and tap it in 3 times with the forefinger and middle finger of your dominant hand.

3. Hold the Groin hand position.

4. Draw the full Reiki sandwich on their solar plexus chakra and tap it in 3 times with the forefinger and middle finger of your dominant hand.

5. Place your hands in the Solar Plexus hand position.

6. Move to your healing partner's head. Draw the full Reiki sandwich on the crown of their head and tap it in 3 times with the forefinger and middle finger of your dominant hand.

7. Hold your hands in the following position sequence: Back of the Head – Ears – Eyes.

8. Move to your healing partner's side. Hold your dominant hand at the crown of your healing partner's head while holding your nondominant hand in the Groin hand position. Visualize energy flowing between your hands.

Tip: Diffuse sandalwood essential oil during the session, as sandalwood facilitates a strong and deep connection to Source energy.

Optimism and Joy

During difficult times, it can be hard to feel optimistic or joyful about anything. However, optimism and joy are associated with love energy, and finding these qualities in ourselves can help us through even the most difficult of times. This sequence can help your healing partner cultivate these qualities in their life.

Affected Chakras

- ► Throat
- ► Heart
- ► Solar plexus

Step-by-Step Instructions

1. Stand at your healing partner's side. Draw the SHK sandwich on your healing partner's heart chakra and tap it in 3 times with the forefinger and middle finger of your dominant hand.

2. Place your hands in the Heart hand position.

3. Move your nondominant hand to the Solar Plexus hand position while keeping your other hand in the Heart hand position.

4. Move your nondominant hand from the Solar Plexus hand position to the Throat hand position while keeping your other hand in the Heart hand position.

5. Return both hands to the Heart hand position once again.

Tip: Play music that contains the 639 Hz solfeggio (many apps and YouTube videos are available) throughout the session to support the opening of heart energy.

Psychic Insight/Intuition

Everyone has the ability to receive intuitive guidance from their higher selves, guides, and Source energy. However, some people have, for whatever reason, blocked that insight or ignored it for so long that it has gone silent. This sequence can help your healing partner reconnect to this very important aspect of self.

Affected Chakras

▸ Crown
▸ Third eye

Step-by-Step Instructions

1. Stand at your healing partner's head. Draw the HSZN sandwich on your healing partner's crown chakra and tap it in 3 times with the forefinger and middle finger of your dominant hand.

2. Draw the HSZN sandwich on your healing partner's third eye chakra and tap it in 3 times with the forefinger and middle finger of your dominant hand.

3. Hold your hands in the Eyes hand position.

4. Hold your hands in the Ears hand position.

5. Place your hands in the Back of the Head hand position.

6. Place your dominant hand on the crown chakra and your nondominant hand on the third eye chakra. Visualize energy flowing between your hands. Hold this bridge position for three minutes, or until you sense release.

Tip: Place an amethyst crystal on either side of your healing partner's head on the table at forehead level to help tune in to intuitive energy.

PART THREE

Third Degree Reiki

Third Degree Reiki is also known as Shinpiden, or Reiki Master-Teacher Degree. In this degree, you will learn to become a Reiki Master-Teacher as well as be attuned to the Reiki Master symbol, called Dai Ko Myo ("Day-koh-MEE-oh"), which allows you to channel the Reiki Master energy. You'll also learn how to teach other people to become Reiki practitioners of all three degrees and how to attune people to the varying degrees of Reiki energy. As always, you'll need to be attuned by a Reiki Master-Teacher to the Reiki Master-Teacher Degree and the Reiki Master symbol in order to activate it.

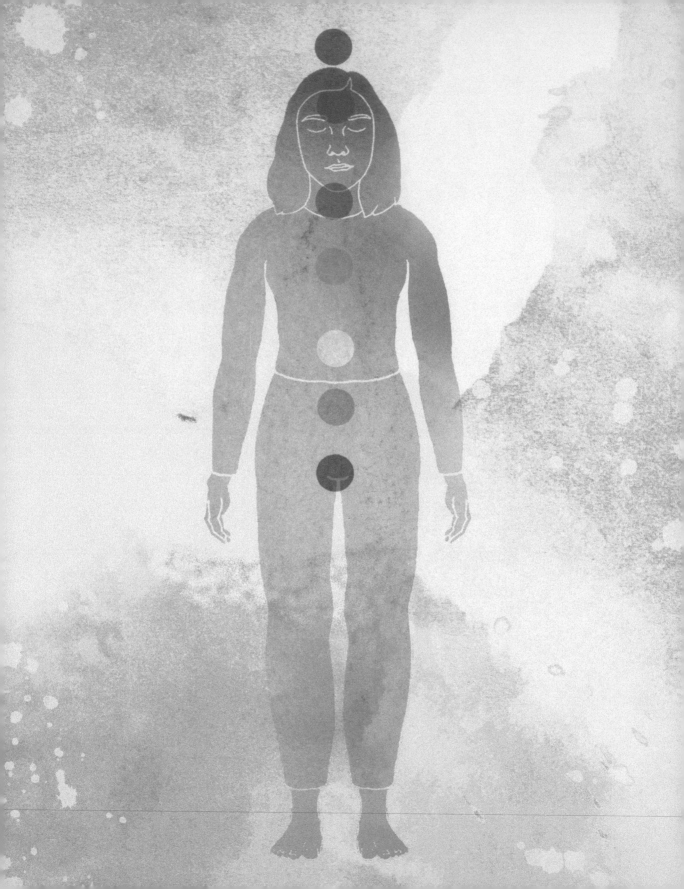

CHAPTER EIGHT

Master-Teacher Reiki Training

In this chapter, you'll learn the basics of becoming a Reiki Master-Teacher, including the Reiki Master-Teacher symbol Dai Ko Myo. We'll also discuss the ethical, spiritual, and practical responsibilities inherent in teaching and attuning others to this powerful healing art.

The Role of a Reiki Master

Many people who seek Reiki Master-Teacher Degree training and attunement do so because they wish to share Reiki with others and initiate them into an empowering healing practice. Those people frequently go on to offer their own Reiki classes and attunements. Others pursue Reiki Master-Teacher Degree for their own purposes, whether it is because they wish to channel a more powerful Reiki energy during their treatments, or because they simply wish to learn as much about Usui Ryoho Reiki as possible. Not everyone chooses to move into the Reiki Master-Teacher Degree energy, so listen to your intuition to discern whether this is right for you.

Spiritual Responsibilities

Because you are a Reiki Master-Teacher, many will look to you as a mentor or teacher. Spiritually, it's your role to help others along their own energy healing journey in a way that serves their greatest good. This involves teaching the spiritual principles associated with the practice of Reiki, such as the five Reiki principles, and related concepts such as meditation, present-time focus, and intention.

Many expect you to step into a role of spiritual leadership in their lives. I believe that once someone learns Reiki from me, I should serve as a source of spiritual support as they navigate their lives as Reiki practitioners. Therefore, I make myself available to students through social media, email, video conferencing, and other methods of contact so I can provide ongoing education and support.

That's the level of spiritual support I choose to offer to my Reiki students. It's up to you to decide as a Reiki Master-Teacher what level of spiritual support you wish to provide. You don't have to be a guru or a spiritual paragon; you are still human. But, to the degree that you feel comfortable, you can serve as a source of spiritual support to your students.

Practical Responsibilities

As a Reiki Master-Teacher, you do have several practical responsibilities:

◆ Teach your students about the history of Usui Ryoho Reiki and the primary figures inherent in its spread to the West.
◆ Provide Reiki training and attunements for all degrees of Reiki.
◆ Provide written materials, such as manuals (you can use this book as a manual) and handouts.
◆ Teach Second Degree and Master-Teacher students the symbols for each degree.
◆ Provide information necessary for each Reiki degree.
◆ Teach ethics and principles associated with each Reiki degree.
◆ Provide Reiki for healing partners.
◆ Teach students to provide Reiki treatments to serve the greatest good.

Traditional Master-Teacher Reiki Symbols

In Usui Ryoho Reiki, one symbol allows you to access the Master-Teacher Degree Reiki energy. This symbol is called Dai Ko Myo. A second symbol is also available for use in Reiki attunements called Raku, although this is a less traditional symbol in Usui Ryoho Reiki. I use Raku in my attunements for grounding.

Dai Ko Myo

SYMBOL AND HOW TO DRAW

 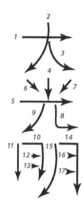

PRONUNCIATION AND ABBREVIATION

Dai Ko Myo is pronounced "Day-koh-MEE-oh"; abbreviated DKM.

MEANING

DKM means "bright shining light." DKM allows you to access and channel Master-Teacher Degree energy. Use DKM in place of all the Second Degree Reiki symbols. Now, instead of using the full Reiki sandwich, for instance, you can simply draw DKM in its place. The exception is during attunements, when you will use the Second Degree symbols as you attune your students to each of them.

MANTRA

Although DKM doesn't have a specific mantra associated with it, when you use it, repeat the symbol name aloud or in your mind's eye three times. When you draw it on your healing partner's body, tap it in three times with your fingers.

WHEN TO USE

◆ During attunements
◆ In place of any and all Second Degree Reiki symbols
◆ To balance energy between body, mind, and spirit
◆ Before meditations to bring Reiki energy into your own meditation practices

ALTERNATE VERSIONS

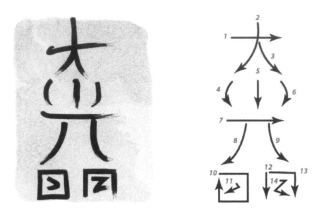

There are several alternative versions of DKM. If one of these versions speaks to you, please feel free to use it in place of DKM.

Raku

SYMBOL AND HOW TO DRAW

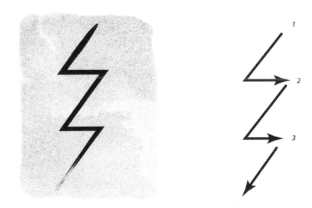

PRONUNCIATION AND ABBREVIATION

Raku is pronounced "Ra-KOO"; not abbreviated.

MEANING

Raku is also known as the "fire serpent" or "fire dragon."

MANTRA

Raku doesn't have a specific mantra associated with it. Repeat the symbol name aloud or in your mind's eye three times when you use it. When you draw it on your healing partner's body, tap it in three times with your fingers.

WHEN TO USE

- At the end of any Reiki session for grounding
- Any time you feel like you need to be grounded
- At the end of a Reiki attunement to ground your student's energy

Nontraditional Reiki Master Symbols

DKM is the traditional Reiki Master symbol in Usui Ryoho Reiki. You'll also find other systems of Reiki that use different Reiki Master symbols or a different set of symbols altogether. For example, in Karuna Ki Reiki, you learn an entirely different set of symbols that are said to go beyond the Reiki Master energy to allow more specific intention.

Attuning Others to Reiki

As a Reiki Master-Teacher, you can attune others to all degrees of Usui Ryoho Reiki energy. I find this role both an honor and a responsibility.

Because Reiki is such a powerful and empowering modality, before you begin teaching and attuning others, you must have a thorough understanding of the principles and pillars of Reiki, the basics of energy anatomy and energy healing, the history and tradition of Reiki, how Reiki works, and the various effects Reiki can have on body, mind, and spirit health.

It's your job as a Reiki Master-Teacher to ensure you thoroughly understand your art and are able to pass it on to your students in an ethical, knowledgeable, and responsible manner. The education your students receive is only as good as how powerfully you've sought to educate yourself, and you owe it to your students to give them a thorough understanding of the art and practice of Reiki before you attune them.

The Reiki attunement ceremony is a sacred moment of shared intention between you and your student. As you attune your students, you connect to them and pass on the intuitive wisdom of Reiki energy on all levels: body, mind, and spirit. These attunement experiences can be profound for both the Reiki Master and the initiate. Many Reiki Masters and their students have shared experiences during attunements such as a psychic or energetic link, intuitive insights, or a profound sense of connection.

Preparation

Reiki attunements can be practical and simple or complex and ceremonial. You can perform them in-person or at a distance, and there are as many different attunement styles and ceremonies as there are Reiki Masters. Typically, I attune my students at the end of each degree of Reiki training with about 30 minutes to an hour left to go in class.

Before I attune my students, I teach the full class, providing them with all the information they need to become Reiki practitioners of whatever degree they are seeking. I leave 30 minutes after attunement for practice. When it is time for attunement, I do the following:

1. Have students take a 10- to 15-minute break. During that time, they step out of the classroom so I can prepare behind closed doors.

2. Arrange chairs in a circle (if they weren't already) with enough room to walk in a full circle around each chair without bumping into anyone.

3. Fill cups for each student with cool water and place one under each chair for grounding at the end of the attunement.

4. Cleanse the room with sage, incense, or palo santo. To do this, light the chosen item and allow it to smolder. Starting at the front door of the room, draw CKR over the front door with the smoldering item, and move around the room in a clockwise direction. In each corner and over each entrance to the room—doors, windows, drains, fireplaces, etc.—draw CKR with the smoldering item.

5. After cleansing, sit in the center of the circle of chairs and draw DKM on your palms. Meditate in Gassho for about five minutes, asking Reiki guides to assist you as you attune new initiates to First, Second, or Master Degree Reiki.

6. Outside the room, ask the students for permission to touch. Bring them into the room, asking them to file in quietly without talking and to sit in their chair with their eyes closed and hands in Gassho.

You may also wish to suggest to your students that in the 24 to 48 hours before their attunement, they do the following:

◆ Avoid intoxicants
◆ Eat light, nutritious meals
◆ Drink plenty of water
◆ Exercise lightly
◆ Get plenty of sleep
◆ Meditate

Hui-Yin

Some Reiki Masters use Hui-Yin in their attunements.

The Hui-Yin point is essentially your perineum (see the image). Some Reiki practitioners believe that by contracting this point (holding it tight), you can create a stronger Reiki circuit for use during attunements. Many feel this strengthens the Reiki energy for the attunement. Some use it during attunements and treatments, whereas others don't. If it speaks to you, please feel free to adopt the practice.

1. Stand behind your healing partner.

2. Contract your Hui-Yin point and place the tip of your tongue on the roof of your mouth. This creates a circuit that allows the Reiki energy to flow through your body in a circular fashion.

3. Visualize a fog of Reiki energy forming around your head. With your Hui-Yin point contracted and your tongue on the roof of your mouth, pull the Reiki energy in through your nose. See it filling your head and flowing in a circuit between the Hui-Yin point and the tip of your tongue.

4. Hold these two points throughout your attunements.

CHAPTER NINE

The Work of a Reiki Master

Many options are available to Reiki Master-Teachers. Some people achieve this degree for the higher vibrational nature of Reiki Master energy, whereas others choose to teach and attune others. Whichever you choose, there are many things you'll need to know as a Reiki Master, including how to develop a curriculum and manual, and how to ensure your practice and teaching of Reiki meets ethical, legal, and spiritual standards.

Licenses and Professional Credentials

Students taught and attuned by a Reiki Master-Teacher have all the credentials they need to practice and teach Reiki and to attune others. To be attuned to Reiki Master energy, you must first be attuned to First Degree and Second Degree Reiki. Seeking credentialing from other professional organizations may also be helpful. Legally, you must meet all requirements for the city, state or province, and country where you'll practice Reiki as a business.

Because various locales have differing requirements for Reiki practitioners, legal requirements may be different. For example, in the state of Washington, where I live and practice, if you practice hands-on Reiki as a business, you must have a valid business license, maintain liability insurance, and have a license to touch, which is a massage therapy license. If you do not have a license to touch, you cannot practice hands-on Reiki healing, but you can hover your hands over your healing partner or practice distance Reiki. However, the state of Washington also grants an exception to the license to touch law for people who practice Reiki as part of their services as an ordained minister. Because I am an ordained metaphysical minister, I am able to practice hands-on Reiki in my practice despite the fact I am not a licensed massage therapist. It's your responsibility to research the requirements in your area, which may vary from city to city, county to county, state to state, and country to country.

Joining a professional Reiki organization may also be helpful to provide an additional layer of credentials. These organizations may offer affordable liability insurance, continuing education, professional journals, and additional credentials for Reiki practitioners.

International Association of Reiki Professionals (IARP)

I belong to the IARP. There is an annual fee for membership, with the option to purchase liability insurance to cover both teaching and practice. The association also offers a quarterly journal and access to ongoing educational materials to expand your knowledge as a Reiki practitioner.

Energy Medicine Professional Association (EMPA)

This professional association covers Reiki practitioners as well as certified practitioners in other forms of energy healing. For a reasonable annual fee, EMPA members have access to liability insurance, research, business tools, and more.

Additional Organizations

Other organizations that may offer helpful credentials, ongoing research, liability insurance, or ordination include:

The International Center for Reiki Training—Credentialing, education, business help, and access to research materials

International Reiki Organization—Networking, marketing support, and ongoing training

International Metaphysical Ministry—Education in metaphysics along with ordination and credentialing through the University of Metaphysics and University of Sedona

Universal Life Church—Ordination and information that may support your practice

Running a Reiki Practice

Many people attuned to Second Degree and Master-Teacher Degree Reiki run their practice as an income-earning business. Many practitioners start small and work their way up, beginning with a part-time, at-home practice before opening a full-time office that generates a livable income.

Business Considerations

Before you quit your day job to become a full-time Reiki practitioner and invest in equipment or a dedicated Reiki space, there are several things to keep in mind. Building a full-time Reiki practice requires a significant investment of time, work, and money. And even once you've built a practice, income can fluctuate. It's up to you to figure out the best way to scale your Reiki practice, to determine when to invest in spaces and equipment, and similar activities.

Setting Up Shop

As a Reiki practitioner providing in-person care, you'll need the following equipment:

◆ A dedicated space with a door where you won't be disturbed
◆ A massage or Reiki table that holds up to 300 pounds safely; adjustable height is beneficial
◆ Sanitizers for cleaning your table and equipment
◆ A filing system for maintaining records
◆ Intake paperwork including HIPAA forms, treatment documentation, and informed consent forms
◆ Some type of audio player (computer, electronic personal assistant, etc.) for playing pleasant music during sessions
◆ Access to a bathroom and cool water

LIABILITY INSURANCE

If you plan to practice or teach Reiki professionally, you must carry liability insurance to protect you, your students, and your healing partners. Depending on how and where you practice, you may need practice insurance as well as liability insurance for the location where you do business.

LICENSING AND TAX REQUIREMENTS

These requirements vary by location, so research to determine what is required to run a Reiki business where you live. Check at the city, county, state, and country level and comply with all licensing and tax requirements.

DOCUMENTATION REQUIREMENTS

In the United States, all health care practitioners, including energy healers, must comply with HIPAA requirements for documentation, confidentiality, and informed consent. Check with your governing bodies to determine what documentation is required, what laws you must follow, and what records to keep. Maintain files for your healing partners and store them in compliance with local, state, and national regulations.

PAYMENT POLICY

Have a written payment policy noting the types of payments you'll accept. In your intake paperwork, have your healing partners sign your payment policy. It's best to run a "cash practice" where healing partners pay for services as rendered. You may also wish to accept credit card payments.

SET FEES

Research to determine the fees that work in your area. I live in a fairly small, rural area, and my fee is $90 for a one-hour session. To arrive at this figure, I did a survey of fees for similar services in my area.

REIKI CERTIFICATION

You must have a certification. Your attunement from a certified Reiki Master-Teacher can serve as your certification, although additional professional credentials can be helpful as well.

Best Practices

Your Reiki practice is a business, but it is also a spiritual and ethical system.

DILIGENTLY RECORD INCOME AND EXPENSES

Ethics are important for energy healing practitioners, so you must keep an ethical, honest, and thorough record of your income and expenses for tax reporting purposes. Keep receipts for expenses and maintain scrupulous records of all payments, including cash payments. Report all income on your tax return.

MAINTAIN CONFIDENTIALITY

A high level of trust is necessary between a health care practitioner and their clients. Maintain confidentiality about anything you learn during your Reiki sessions as well as anything that happens there.

NEVER DIAGNOSE

Legally, you cannot diagnose your healing partners, and it's important that you don't offer anything that could be interpreted as a diagnosis during your sessions. If you notice something during a session, instead of reporting that to your healing partner (which might be interpreted as a diagnosis), instead suggest your healing partner seek medical evaluation.

NEVER COUNTERACT A DOCTOR'S ORDERS

You should never appear to counteract, or even judge, the advice, orders, diagnoses, or other information a healing partner receives from their primary health care practitioner. Remain in a neutral, nonjudgmental space during your sessions.

INTEND FOR REIKI TO SERVE THE GREATEST GOOD

During a Reiki session, avoid imposing your agenda onto your healing partner. Always enter into Reiki treatment with the goal of serving your healing partner's greatest good.

ASK PERMISSION TO TOUCH

Ask permission to touch at the beginning of every Reiki session, even with healing partners who have granted that permission before. If you suspect certain hand positions may be triggering for a healing partner, ask about those specific positions. Only send distance Reiki with permission from your distance healing partner.

Developing a Reiki Training Curriculum

As a Reiki Master-Teacher, you may feel called upon to teach students. Before you begin teaching, do everything you can to familiarize yourself with the Reiki energy and to become intimately acquainted with the principles and techniques associated with Usui Ryoho Reiki. The more you know and the better you understand your material, the better teacher you will be.

Teaching Philosophy and Style

Before teaching others, make sure you have a set philosophy about Reiki and how you will teach it. I can't tell you what your teaching philosophy or style should be, but I can share mine to help you understand how to develop your own. Adapt my philosophy to fit your own framework.

- Establish a safe space during Reiki classes. Establish the classroom as a safe space free from judgment, so students feel safe to share and ask questions. Do this at the outset of class by asking all students to agree to a nonjudgmental, open, safe space and promise to maintain the confidentiality of other students.
- At the outset, outline expectations for asking questions, taking breaks, etc. Give a brief overview of how the class will go, when you will attune, etc.
- Maintain an intimate knowledge of what you teach. Know the materials and make sure you've worked with the energy and healing partners enough to understand how various people react to Reiki.
- Continue your own education.
- Allow time for practice during classes.

Course Materials

This book is a great starting point to develop your own course materials. You can use it as your Reiki manual or develop your own. The information provided in this book provides a good outline of the information you'll need to teach for each degree.

FIRST DEGREE

At minimum, teach or provide the following:

◆ Reiki history including Usui Sensei, Dr. Hayashi, and Mrs. Takata
◆ Reiki lineage
◆ Five principles of Reiki
◆ How Reiki energy works
◆ Hand positions for self-treatment and treating others
◆ First Degree Reiki manual
◆ First Degree Reiki attunement

SECOND DEGREE

At minimum, teach or provide the following:

◆ Review of First Degree principles
◆ Three Pillars of Reiki
◆ Second Degree Reiki symbols—CKR, DKM, and HSZN—and how to use them
◆ How to perform distance treatments using symbols
◆ Second Degree manual
◆ Second Degree attunement, including attunement to the symbols

REIKI MASTER-TEACHER

At minimum, teach or provide the following:

◆ Review of First and Second Degree principles
◆ Reiki Master symbol—DKM—and how to use it
◆ How to perform attunements
◆ Reiki Master-Teacher manual
◆ Reiki Master-Teacher attunement

Teaching Space

You can teach and attune in-person or online. I prefer to teach in-person because it allows my students time to practice their skills after attunement. I allow at least 30 minutes of hands-on practice. This isn't possible in distance classes, but

I have students from all around the world, so I offer live online classes via video conferencing, too.

I can teach Reiki classes in my home office, but I prefer to rent a space with parking. I've rented various spaces at rec centers, churches, conference centers, and more. Because I travel to teach, I have portable tables. If you plan to teach in-person classes outside of your normal space, consider lightweight tables that are easy to pack and transport.

The Master-Student Relationship

My goal as a Reiki Master-Teacher is to foster an open, nonjudgmental, and supportive relationship with my students. I encourage them to work with me if they feel the energy between us is good, but if they aren't feeling the connection, to work with a Reiki Master-Teacher with whom they do feel more connected.

As a Master-Teacher, you are there to serve as an educator, mentor, and source of encouragement. Make yourself available outside of the classroom, as many questions arise after students have had their training when they're practicing in the real world.

As a mentor, it's also your job to work with your students ethically. Model the behaviors you ask of your students and always keep communications open yet confidential.

Exploring Reiki Further

As a Reiki Master-Teacher, the more you know, the better you can support your students and healing partners. Therefore, I strongly encourage you to become a lifelong Reiki learner (see the Resources on page 211).

- ◆ Read Reiki journals and articles.
- ◆ Read books about Reiki and other forms of energy healing or energy anatomy.
- ◆ Learn additional forms of Reiki. If you feel drawn to other types of Reiki, then take the course and receive the attunement.
- ◆ Learn about other forms of energy healing.

CHAPTER TEN

Reiki Attunements

Basic Ceremonial Attunement (In-Person)

When I attune students in-person, I always ask if they'd prefer a ceremonial attunement or a quick attunement. Both accomplish attunement, but I find that many students prefer some ceremony during attunement. The ceremonial attunement takes about five minutes per student, and it's efficient enough that you can use it with groups. When working with a group, have them sit in a circle and attune each student individually. Prepare the space before the attunement as indicated on page 174.

Preparation for Groups

Once the room is prepared, invite the group to silently file in and sit in their chair with their hands in Gassho at heart level and their eyes closed throughout the ceremony. Note that when it is their turn, you will touch them on the shoulder to let them know they are being attuned, and if their arms get tired in Gassho, they can lower their hands to their lap and you will lift them into place when it is their turn. Once everyone is seated in Gassho, invite them to silently indicate their willingness to receive a First, Second, or Master Degree Reiki attunement, and ask the first person you are attuning to indicate their readiness after doing this by nodding their head.

Step-by-Step Instructions

This is the basic attunement you will use for all three degrees. Insert the word for the proper degree where there's a choice of words and use the variations for each degree in the subheads below the basic steps.

1. With your finger, draw DKM on both of your palms.

2. Stand facing your student with your hands in Gassho. Once your student has indicated their readiness for attunement by nodding, close your eyes and say in your mind: "I invite all Reiki Masters past, present, and future including Usui Sensei, Dr. Hayashi, and Mrs. Takata to help me as I attune (student's name) to First/Second/Master Degree Reiki."

3. Walk around your student to stand behind them, touching them lightly on the shoulder to let them know it's their turn.

4. With the pointer finger of your dominant hand, in the air above your student's crown chakra, draw DKM.

5. Hold both hands above their crown chakra. Visualize Reiki energy flowing from your hands and into their crown chakra, moving downward into every cell of their body. Hold until you feel ready to move (usually about 30 seconds to 1 minute).

6. Walk around your student to the front. Using the forefinger of your dominant hand, draw DKM in the air a few inches in front their third eye chakra.

7. Cup both hands and hold them in front of student's third eye, visualizing Reiki energy flowing from your hands into the chakra.

8. Using the forefinger of your dominant hand, draw DKM in the air a few inches in front of their throat chakra.

9. Cup both hands and hold them in front of your student's throat chakra, visualizing Reiki energy flowing into the chakra.

10. Lower your student's hands to their lap.

11. Using the forefinger of your dominant hand, draw DKM in the air a few inches in front of the heart chakra.

12. Cup both hands and hold them in front the heart chakra, visualizing Reiki energy flowing from your hands into the chakra.

13. Using the forefinger of your dominant hand, draw DKM in the air a few inches in front of your student large enough so it covers the solar plexus, sacral, and root chakras.

14. Cup both of your hands and hold them in front of your student's solar plexus, visualizing Reiki energy flowing from your hands into the remaining chakras.

15. Gently lift your student's hands so they are back in front of their heart.

16. Draw Raku in front of your student from head to toe, touching the ground at the end.

17. Step back and stand in Gassho. In your mind, say, "(Name) is now attuned to First/Second/Master Degree Reiki. I give thanks to all Reiki Masters, past, present, and future including Usui Sensei, Dr. Hayashi, and Mrs. Takata for assisting in this attunement and affirm that (name) will move forward as a powerful and confident First/Second/Master Degree Reiki practitioner."

18. Invite your student to express, in their mind, gratitude for their attunement to First/Second/Master Degree Reiki. If in a group, do this and the following steps after you've attuned everyone.

19. Invite your student(s) to open their eyes and offer them a glass of cold water for grounding.

20. Step away to run your hands under cold water to break the bond between you and your student(s).

Second Degree Variation

1. Complete steps 1–14 of the basic attunement.

2. Open your student's hands. With the forefinger of your dominant hand, draw CKR on the student's right palm, saying it in your mind 3 times, and tap the symbol into their palm with 3 taps using your forefinger and middle finger. Do the same on their left palm.

3. Draw SHK on the student's right palm, saying it in your mind 3 times, and tap the symbol into their palm with 3 taps using your forefinger and middle finger. Do the same on their left palm.

4. Draw HSZN on the student's right palm, saying it in your mind 3 times, and tap the symbol into their palm with 3 taps using your forefinger and middle finger. Do the same on their left palm.

5. Continue with steps 15–20 of the basic attunement.

Master-Teacher Degree Variation

1. Complete steps 1–14 of the basic attunement.

2. Open your student's hands. With the forefinger of your dominant hand, draw DKM on the student's right palm, saying it in your mind 3 times, and tap the symbol into their palm with 3 taps using your forefinger and middle finger. Do the same on their left palm.

3. Continue with steps 15–20 of the basic attunement.

Basic Fast Attunement (In-Person)

Occasionally, I have a student request the quick attunement. This is also known as a crown-to-crown attunement, and it works through the power of intention. This takes just a minute or two per student.

Preparation for Groups

Preparation for groups is the same as the ceremonial attunement.

Step-by-Step Instructions

This is the basic attunement you will use for all three degrees. Insert the word for the proper degree where there's a choice of words and use the variations for each degree in the subheads below the basic steps.

1. With your finger, draw DKM on both of your palms.

2. Sit or stand facing your student with your hands in Gassho. Once your student has indicated their readiness for attunement by nodding, close your eyes and say in your mind: "I invite all Reiki Masters past, present, and future including Usui Sensei, Dr. Hayashi, and Mrs. Takata to help me as I attune (student's name) to First/Second/Master Degree Reiki."

3. Visualize Reiki pouring down from above you into your crown chakra and beaming out of your third eye and into your student's third eye, where it fills their entire body with Reiki energy.

4. Maintain this position until you can visualize your student's entire body filled with Reiki energy (usually about 30 seconds to 1 minute).

5. In your mind, say, "(Name) is now attuned to First/Second/Master Degree Reiki. I give thanks to all Reiki Masters, past, present, and future including Usui Sensei, Dr. Hayashi, and Mrs. Takata for assisting in this attunement and affirm that (name) will move forward as a powerful and confident First/Second/Master Degree Reiki practitioner."

6. Draw Raku in front of your student from head to toe, touching the ground at the end.

7. If you're attuning a group, continue around the circle to each student until all have been attuned.

8. Invite your student to express, in their mind, gratitude for their attunement to First/Second/Master Degree Reiki. If in a group, do this and the following steps after you've attuned everyone.

9. Invite your student(s) to open their eyes and offer them a glass of cold water for grounding.

10. Step away to run your hands under cold water to break the bond between you and your student(s).

Second Degree Variation

1. Complete steps 1–4 of the basic attunement.

2. Lower your student's hands to their lap and open their hands. With the forefinger of your dominant hand, draw CKR on the student's right palm, saying it in your mind 3 times, and tap the symbol into their palm with 3 taps using your forefinger and middle finger. Do the same on their left palm.

3. Draw SHK on the student's right palm, saying it in your mind 3 times, and tap the symbol into their palm with 3 taps using your forefinger and middle finger. Do the same on their left palm.

4. Draw HSZN on the student's right palm, saying it in your mind 3 times, and tap the symbol into the palm with 3 taps using your forefinger and middle finger. Do the same on their left palm.

5. Continue with steps 5–10 of the basic attunement.

Master-Teacher Degree Variation

1. Complete steps 1–4 of the Second Degree attunement.

2. Lower your student's hands to their lap and open their hands. With the forefinger of your dominant hand, draw DKM on the student's right palm, saying it in your mind 3 times, and tap the symbol into their palm with 3 taps using your forefinger and middle finger. Do the same on their left palm.

3. Continue with steps 5–10 of the basic attunement.

Basic Distance Attunement (All Degrees)

If you're conducting a First Degree attunement at a distance, you'll use a surrogate in place of your students. I use a small teddy bear, but you can use any doll or stuffed animal in place of the student. Set a time with your student for the attunement and invite them to spend about 15 minutes at the designated time with their hands held in Gassho at heart level and their eyes closed. Additionally, tell your student that as soon as they sit down in Gassho, they should silently indicate their willingness to be attuned to First/Second/Master Degree Reiki.

Step-by-Step Instructions

1. Go somewhere you won't be disturbed at your preset time.

2. With your finger, draw DKM on both of your palms.

3. In your mind's eye or aloud, state that the surrogate is a stand-in for (student's name) in their attunement to First/Second/Master Degree Reiki.

4. Hold the surrogate in your lap, and using either the ceremonial or quick attunement, perform all the steps for First, Second, or Master Degree attunement on the surrogate.

Adding the Violet Breath to Attunements

Some Reiki Master-Teachers also like to add an additional ceremonial element to all degrees of attunement called the violet breath. *This is not an attunement I do because I am uncomfortable blowing air on my students. Performing the violet breath adds an additional layer of ceremony, but the results remain the same. If you do decide to use it, please make sure you let your students know it is coming so they aren't startled by the violet breath.*

Step-by-Step Instructions

1. Perform the specified attunement as noted in the instructions on the preceding pages. Before the final step—where you sit in front of your student and affirm they are now a Reiki practitioner (after tapping the symbols into the hands and sending Reiki into each of the chakras)—move around to the back of your student again so you are standing behind them.

2. Contract your Hui-Yin point and place the tip of your tongue on the roof of your mouth. Hold this position throughout all the steps that follow.

3. Close your eyes and visualize violet light flowing all around you.

4. Take three deep cleansing breaths, in through your nose for a full 3 seconds, and then exhale for a full 3 seconds.

5. Then take a full, deep breath. See the violet light entering through your breath and swirling around inside your head, filling your full body, including your lungs.

6. When you have breathed in as much violet light as possible, exhale it through your mouth, blowing it into your student's crown chakra. See the violet light flow out of you and fill your student, flowing from their crown chakra down to permeate their entire body.

7. Remove your tongue from the roof of your mouth and uncontract your Hui-Yin point.

8. Finish the attunement as directed.

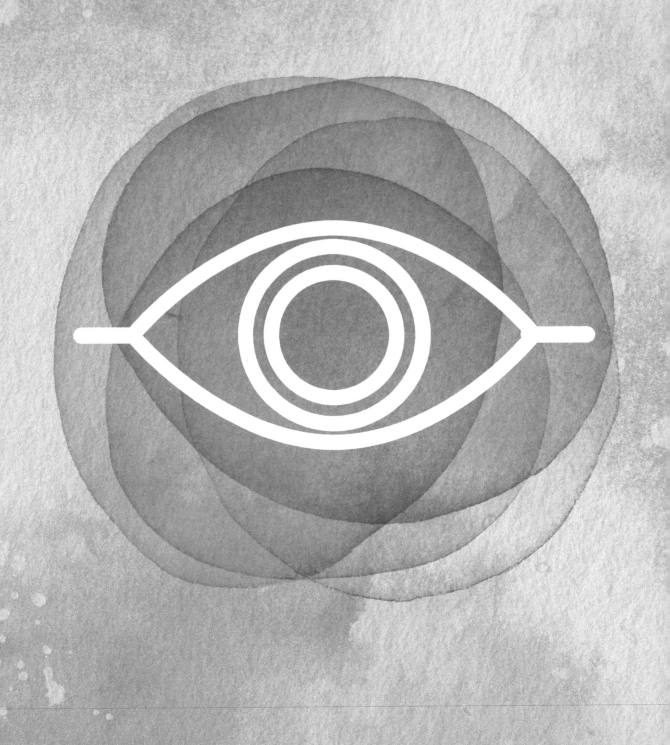

Additional Hand Positions

Adrenal Balance

Adrenal glands are located on either side of the body atop the kidneys. They release the stress hormones responsible for the fight, flight, or freeze response. In today's stressful world, the adrenal glands frequently have to work overtime and can become fatigued or overactive. I use the adrenals hand position with virtually every healing partner because I believe everyone's adrenals could use a little work.

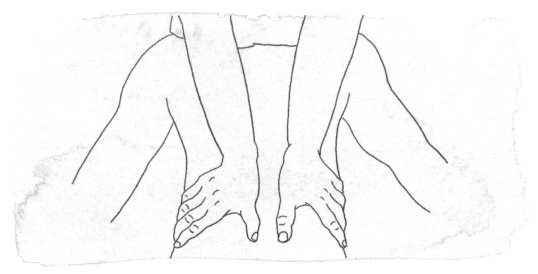

1. Have your healing partner lie on their stomach.

2. Stand at their head.

3. Place the palm of each hand directly over their adrenal glands (tops of kidneys) with the fingers of each hand extending out to the sides.

4. Hold for three to five minutes, or until you sense or notice signs of release.

Arthritis Joint Cupping

If your healing partner has arthritis or pain of a specific joint, use joint cupping on any joint that has pain. Be sure to use a light touch so you don't increase the pain with too much pressure.

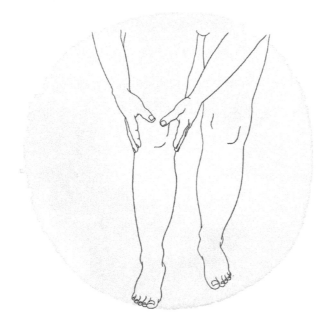

1. Have your healing partner sit or lie comfortably on their back.

2. Hold your hands lightly cupped, with your thumbs touching if possible.

3. Place one hand on either side of their joint.

4. Hold for three to five minutes, or until you sense or notice signs of release.

Autoimmune Bridge Position

The autoimmune bridge position involves holding your dominant hand over your healing partner's root chakra and your nondominant hand over the organ or area affected by the autoimmune disease. For example, for Hashimoto's thyroiditis or Graves' disease, hold your nondominant hand over their neck. For autoimmune diseases such as multiple sclerosis or scleroderma, hold your nondominant hand at their crown chakra.

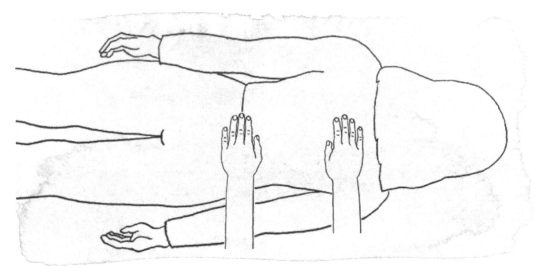

1. Have your healing partner lie on their stomach. Stand to the side.

2. Place your dominant hand over their tailbone.

3. Place your nondominant hand over the organ or area affected.

4. Hold for three to five minutes, or until you sense or notice signs of release.

Baby Balance

Babies have tiny bodies and don't require much Reiki before they're filled up. Because they are so small, you can balance a baby's energy quickly using this easy baby balance hand position.

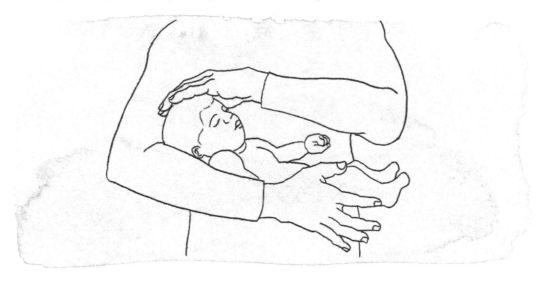

1. Sit comfortably.

2. Cradle the baby in your arms, with one hand cupping the baby's bottom and the baby resting safely in your arms.

3. Place your other hand on the top of the baby's head.

4. Hold for three to five minutes, or until the baby starts to squirm.

Baby Colic

For a colicky baby, you can use a simple hand position to soothe the gas pains.

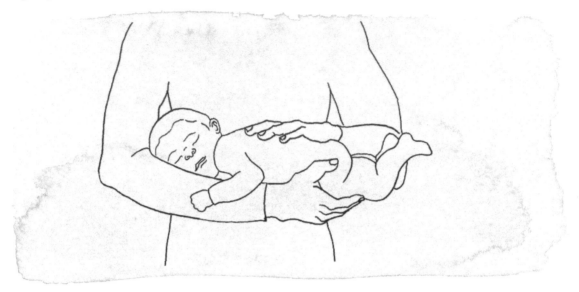

1. Sit holding the baby in your lap across your knees, either facedown or faceup.

2. Place one hand under the baby's stomach and the other hand on the baby's back.

3. Hold for three to five minutes, or until the baby starts to squirm.

Back Pain Bridge Position

For healing partners suffering from back pain, you can hold a bridge position to send energy through the spine and muscles to create a relaxation response.

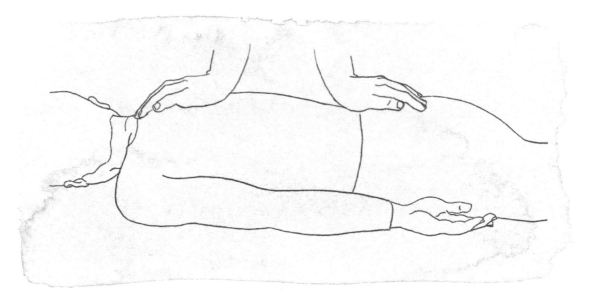

1. Have your healing partner lie on their stomach. Place a bolster beneath their hips if it increases their comfort.

2. Place one hand lightly along their spine between their shoulder blades.

3. Place your other hand along their spine just above their buttocks.

4. Hold for three to five minutes, or until you sense or notice signs of release.

Dental Pain Position

For people suffering from dental or mouth pain, such as canker sores, this hand position can help supply soothing energy to provide temporary relief until your healing partner can make it to a dentist.

1. Have your healing partner lie on their back.

2. Hold your hands so the heels are together, and your fingers extend outward toward their cheeks.

3. Place your hands lightly over their mouth (or hover), cupping your fingers around the curve of their face toward their cheeks.

4. Hold for three to five minutes, or until your healing partner indicates they feel some relief.

Headache Bridge Position

This position works well for any headache, but especially for tension headaches with accompanying neck pain or stiffness. Perform with your healing partner sitting or lying down.

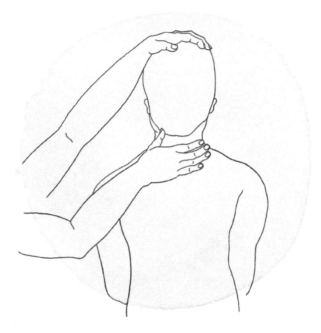

1. Have your healing partner lie on their stomach or sit with their back toward you.

2. Place one hand at the base of their neck, with your fingers extending along one side of their neck and your thumb extending to the other.

3. Place your other hand on the crown of their head.

4. Visualize energy flowing between your hands as you hold for three to five minutes, or until your healing partner indicates they feel some relief.

Kidney Pain Position

For healing partners suffering from pain associated with the kidneys and urinary tract—such as kidney stones, kidney infection, or urinary tract pain—this hand position can bring relief. Please make sure that with such serious health issues, your healing partner is also seeking care from a physician.

1. Have your healing partner lie on their side with their knees bent and their affected side up. Stand to the side.

2. Place the heel of one hand just over their kidney, with your fingers extending toward their spine.

3. Place your other hand along their spine, with the heel of your hand just under where the bra line would be, extending down the spine.

4. Use a light touch to avoid aggravating pain.

5. Hold for three to five minutes, or until your healing partner indicates they feel some relief.

Small Pets Allover Reiki

If you have a small pet—such as a cat, small dog, or rabbit—you can channel Reiki to them with a single hand position. This is a great way to channel Reiki to small, tame animals.

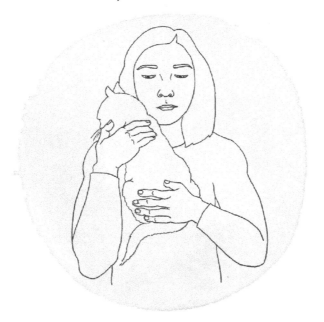

1. Sit with your pet cradled in your lap or against your chest.

2. Place one hand on your pet's bottom/flank.

3. Place your other hand on your pet's head.

4. Hold for three to five minutes, or until your pet indicates it is done receiving the energy (by squirming or trying to get away).

5. If your pet isn't having it, try again another time.

Resources

Books

Anatomy of the Spirit: The Seven Stages of Power and Healing by Caroline Myss

If you're looking for a primer that shows how energy affects health, this is the one to get. Medical intuitive Caroline Myss walks you through each chakra and shows you how imbalances in the chakras can affect health.

The Art of Psychic Reiki: Developing Your Intuitive and Empathic Abilities for Energy Healing by Lisa Campion

If you want to incorporate your intuition into your Reiki practice, this book teaches you how. It discusses how to nurture your intuition and develop your empathetic abilities.

Crystal Reiki: A Handbook for Healing Mind, Body, and Soul by Krista N. Mitchell

If you want to add crystals to your Reiki practice, this book is a great guide to get you started in adding the energy healing effects of crystals to your Reiki practice.

An Evidence Based History of Reiki by William Lee Rand

If you want to learn the history of Reiki, this book will help you discern between legend and truth.

The Original Reiki Handbook of Dr. Mikao Usui by Mikao Usui and Christine M. Grimm

If you want to go to the source, this book shares Reiki as Usui Sensei meant it to be. This resource should be on every Reiki practitioner's shelf.

Reiki Healing for Beginners: The Practical Guide with Remedies for 100+ Ailments by Karen Frazier

If you're just starting out, this book will help you learn the basics of Reiki. It contains healing sequences for more than 100 ailments.

The Subtle Body: An Encyclopedia of Your Energetic Anatomy by Cyndi Dale

If you want to learn the energy anatomy associated with the human body, this reference guide outlines this anatomy, including auras, chakras, and meridians.

The Subtle Body Coloring Book by Cyndi Dale

If you learn better from hands-on practice, this coloring book is a helpful resource. Think of it as an anatomy coloring book for chakras, auras, and meridians.

Websites

International Association of Reiki Professionals: IARP.org

This site offers Reiki professionals tons of resources, such as manuals, certificates, a Reiki journal, and more.

The International Center for Reiki Training: Reiki.org

This is a well-respected Reiki education site that teaches you about all aspects of Reiki and offers great resources for all degrees of Reiki practitioners.

Reiki Rays: ReikiRays.com

This site is a great source of ongoing education for Reiki practitioners, with free ebook downloads, articles, and other fantastic resources to further your Reiki education.

References

American Association for the Advancement of Science (AAAS). "Einstein's 'Spooky Action at a Distance' Spotted in Objects Almost Big Enough to See." *Science*. April 25, 2018. ScienceMag.org/news/2018/04/einstein-s -spooky-action-distance-spotted-objects-almost-big-enough-see.

American Autoimmune Related Diseases Association, Inc. (AARDA). "Auto-immune Disease List." Accessed May 16, 2020. AARDA.org/diseaselist.

American Chronic Pain Association (ACPA). "Quick Facts on Fibromyalgia." Accessed May 16, 2020. TheACPA.org/conditions-treatments /conditions-a-z/fibromyalgia/two-takes-on-fibro/quick-facts-on -fibromyalgia.

Anxiety and Depression Association of America (ADAA). "Facts & Statistics." Accessed May 16, 2020. ADAA.org/about-adaa/press-room/facts -statistics.

Centers for Disease Control and Prevention. "Arthritis: How CDC Improves Quality of Life for People With Arthritis." Accessed May 16, 2020. CDC.gov/chronicdisease/resources/publications/factsheets/arthritis.htm.

Cleveland Clinic. "Anxiety Disorders." Accessed May 16, 2020. my.ClevelandClinic.org/health/diseases/9536-anxiety-disorders.

Mayo Clinic "Metabolic Syndrome: Symptoms & Causes." March 14, 2019. MayoClinic.org/diseases-conditions/metabolic-syndrome/symptoms -causes/syc-20351916.

Migraine Research Foundation "Migraine Facts." Accessed May 16, 2020.
    MigraineResearchFoundation.org/about-migraine/migraine-facts.

National Institute of Diabetes and Digestive and Kidney Diseases (NIDDK).
    "Definition & Facts of Indigestion." Accessed May 16, 2020.
    NIDDK.nih.gov/health-information/digestive-diseases/indigestion
    -dyspepsia/definition-facts.

World Health Organization (WHO). "Hypertension." Accessed May 16, 2020.
    WHO.int/news-room/fact-sheets/detail/hypertension.

Index

Acknowledgments

Writing a book about energy healing during a worldwide pandemic reminds me just how important and necessary energy healing modalities such as Reiki are for the world. I am so grateful to all who have been an essential part of my Reiki healing journey, including my Reiki Masters Howard Batie and Lisa Powers and all those who have taught me about various forms of energy healing over the years.

I'd also like to thank my husband, Jim, and my two adult children, Tanner and Liz, who have for years put up with how absorbed I can become in my work as both a writer and energy healer. I'm also extremely grateful to my business partners at the Vision Collective for helping me find my spiritual family and a place to share this wonderful healing art with others, including Jason and Carolyn Masuoka, Kristen Gray, Sharon Lewis, Luis Navarrete, Mackenna Long, Tristan David Luciotti, and Seth Michael. Thanks also to Cheryl Knight and Chad Wilson, who were the first to allow me a place to write about energy healing and whose friendship and encouragement continue to inspire me. I also wish to thank all of my family—both my family of birth and my family of choice; there are too many of you to name and I'm always afraid I'll forget someone, but I trust you know who you are.

I'm also incredibly grateful to Callisto Media and the publishing team there, especially Clara Song Lee, who was my first editor/project manager; Stacy Wagner-Kinnear, with whom I've collaborated on a number of projects; and Andrea Leptinsky, who served as the editor on this book.

Finally, thanks to the hundreds of students I've been privileged enough to teach over the years and the many healing partners who have trusted me to work with them. I am incredibly humbled by the trust you have placed in me.

About the Author

Karen Frazier is an intuitive energy healer, Reiki Master-Teacher, ordained metaphysical minister, psychic medium, and author. She has worked with and attuned hundreds of healing partners and students and has written numerous books about energy healing, crystals, and Reiki.

Along with being an Usui Ryoho Reiki Master-Teacher, Karen is a Crystal Reiki Master, Animal Reiki Master, Karuna Ki Reiki Master, and Raku Reiki Master. She offers a number of energy healing services along with Reiki, including sound healing, metaphysical healing, polarity therapy, crystal healing, astrological herbalism, and neurolinguistic programming (NLP).

Karen writes an energy healing column and a dream interpretation column for *Paranormal Underground Magazine,* hosts the *Intention Is Everything Podcast*, and writes and edits articles about energy healing, tarot, astrology, and feng shui for the website LoveToKnow. She is a member of the Vision Collective, the International Metaphysical Ministry, and the International Association of Reiki Professionals, and she holds advanced degrees in metaphysics and energy healing. Learn more at AuthorKarenFrazier.com.

CPSIA information can be obtained
at www.ICGtesting.com
Printed in the USA
JSHW011908280122
22324JS00004B/4

9 781647 398194